Subconscious Journeys

Jack Mitchell

Hamilton Books

A member of
Rowman & Littlefield
Lanham • Boulder • New York • Toronto • Plymouth, UK

Copyright © 2014 by Hamilton Books
4501 Forbes Boulevard, Suite 200, Lanham, Maryland 20706
Hamilton Books Aquisitions Department (301) 459-3366

10 Thornbury Road, Plymouth PL6 7PP, United Kingdom

Library of Congress Control Number: 2013957835
ISBN: 978-0-7618-6333-5 (paperback : alk. paper)—ISBN: 978-0-7618-6334-2
(elec-tronic)

Contents

Foreword

The purpose for writing *Subconscious Journeys* was intensified when my emotionally distraught twenty-three-year-old son killed himself. Scott was a gentle, sensitive, young man who grew up aware that he had been adopted. Seemingly, he suspected he was abandoned by his birth mother because he was unwanted.

Scott never recovered emotionally, doubting others could really love him. Not only was I Scott's adopted father, but also a practicing therapist. I recognized the symptoms of his nervous irritability, bouts of moodiness, and chronic depression. When working with my son in therapy failed, I referred him to a colleague. There, Scott found some initial therapeutic relief, then spiraled steadily downward.

Following his wife's infidelity, most of Scott's martial problems were aggravated by and erupted during bouts of alcohol abuse. The concoction of alcohol, depression, and a deeply rooted poor self-esteem became lethal to my son. In 1988 Scott committed suicide after his wife left him following a martial altercation.

Preface

Our immortality quest is limited and controlled largely by our life expectancy and personalities. Although lives have been extended by scientific and medical advances, the rewards are vastly exceeded by that of human's emotionally motivated wants and desires, reminiscent of Spanish explorer Juan Ponce Deleon's (14060-1521) search for the legendary *Fountain of Youth*. Increasingly, there is a growing clamor for instant cures, youthful serums, and miracle potions to extend life beyond its present limits.

How is it that some individuals live longer and sustain healthier lives? Why does one individual survive a catastrophe, while another succumbs to a similar situation? Superior physical condition? Or do some individuals have the ability to think their way to longer lives? The answers and solutions have enticed and eluded scholars and our earliest ancestors since time's beginning.

Yet the answers are not right under, but above and behind our noses, encapsulated in the most complex and compound computer ever devised: the human mind. We need look no further. We have—no—we ARE the answer. Each and every one of us possesses the innate ability to extend or end our respective lives. We may be enriched and experience enjoyable heights, or plummet to suffer life's miseries. It's simply a matter of choices. They are, and have always been ours, for they are locked within our minds, and each one of us holds the key to open ourselves to enjoy life's greatest pleasures. Such are not worldly acclaim, for what good is acclamation without inner peace, a sense of a loving acceptance towards one's self and others? Yet this harmonious state can only be obtained when we learn how to release the negative emotions that are frequently harbored for a lifetime. Shakespeare wrote, "aye, there's the rub." The mystery has been solved: WE are our own enemy. But what's the solution? Read on.

Introduction

After approximately thirty research years, which included the author's personal therapy, he has come to write *Subconscious Journeys*. The research was a personal task aimed at a graduate degree; the therapy was an endeavor to create changes within his own life and mind. Accordingly, he experienced personal behavior improvements and witnessed those same changes in others, who took the same journey.

Subconscious Journey explores modern society's increasing dependence upon wholesale quackeries, instant cures, and unreliable or invalidated medications that treat symptoms of causes, and conduct unnecessary research, becoming rich in the process. A medically dominated society not only depends, but increasingly thrives upon wholesale quackcrics, instant cures, and instant remedies.

Modern-day society envisions itself as being enlightened, yet its members flee from emotional self-analysis and seek a myriad of elixirs. It's the author's aim to prescribe a more realistic and effective antidote. The remedy is astonishingly quite simple: enlightenment. It will not only enrich, but extend, make your life more meaningful, and release peacefulness and altruism.

Subconscious Journey's penetrates the human mind, the most complex computer ever devised. Since time's beginning, humans have been awed by its ability.

The author was about twenty-five when first introduced to the term "neurosis." The startling word eventually led to a lengthy personal journey of working on a graduate degree, studying and researching, and personal therapeutic endeavors while working with a scholar and friend, Doctor Milton Alvis.

This journey changed the author from one who exploded easily, to a person of calmness. A sexually aggressive, self-focused person; who became a caring individual, who has at last able to empathize with others' needs and relinquish his own.

The wonderful changes in attitude and behavior enabled the author to overcome rheumatoid arthritis, asthma, allergies, heart trouble, prostatitis, and other organic problems.

Subsequently, the author worked with others while using those same methods: learning how to release aggressiveness and selfishness, and embrace peacefulness and altruism. The student not only drew upon the mentoring teacher's resources, but was able to employ his own personality, and experiences throughout his personal therapy; thereby, deriving organic changes.

Having witnessed these beneficial changes in patients' lives; as they, too, broke free of the chains of self-destructive attitudes and behaviors, the author was reminded of the immortal words of Doctor Martin Luther King, Jr.: "Free at last, Free at last. Thank You God Almighty. I'm free at last." So, too, were the author's patients when they tamed their personal emotional tigers. One said, "The weight of the world has been removed from my shoulder." And another, "Now I don't have to worry what I might do next." What a gratifying journey we all have!

Chapter One

The Human Mind

The human mind is essentially divided into four parts, and *Subconscious Journeys* will explore the Conscious, the Subconscious, the Conscience, and the Personality.

The subconscious lies below the conscious and stores much that affects every animal's life. The personality is housed within the subconscious and is exhibited throughout all behavior and attitudes. The final mind part, the Conscience lies within the subconscious and directs most conscious thoughts. These categories will be discussed later.

But, the mind's demarcations frequently lack definitive separations. The conscious and subconscious thoughts inter-blend within the more shallow conscious and subconscious levels. As conscious thoughts and subconsciously derived emotions easily interchange. Personalities, entirely controlled by the conscience, are developed largely through pleasant and unpleasant experiences. As individuals age, the mind-part separations become more pronounced, and the semi-rigid, conscience-controls become more severe. Yet, if the strong emotions are removed, the lines are easily crossed from the subconscious to the conscious. Accordingly, ongoing, instant changes are experienced throughout the mind, and if the four parts do exist independently, departmentally, their coordinated, complete

functions blend conjunctionally within most well adjusted personalities.

Most studies have been aimed exclusively at the conscious
mind. In an initial glance, the conscious exhibits both normal and
abnormal behaviors, and personalities live and strive within their
boundaries, and in their limitations, life's challenges are met.
Therein, too, great religions are embraced; within them consciously
exhibited neurotic behavior is somewhat controlled and corrected.

Therapies have mostly been conducted in and aimed at conscious behaviors while treating subconsciously born conscientiously induced neurotic behaviors; many are called counseling movements. Obviously, the conscious is the easiest in which to counsel
and teach, as many scholars, through inexperience, ignore the subconscious. Frequently, moral lectures are employed to correct abnormal behavior. The author frequently observed graduate students
and teachers counseling patients on neurotic behavior, while both
the students and teachers exhibited the same subconsciously induced neurotic trends.

Above it all, life's miracle is real, and it resides within the mind.
It's complicated because personalities live within physical bodies
and direct movement somewhat through thought patterns.

And they consciously exhibit personality characteristics, which
identify them throughout life. Unfortunately, the consciously exhibited neurotic behaviors are subconsciously formed and conscientiously directed. Those characteristics limit and identify individuals as they habitually address issues and set patterns that char-
acterize every personality developmental stage. They thereby establish identities, change images (individual physical changes), ad
establish limits through subconsciously induced-identification
thought patterns. They simply adopt more identification characteristics, and become more like themselves because humans are habit-
forming creatures; the thought patterns are frequently repeated by
both chance and design. In younger years, within the personality

forming cycle, free unemotional choice is probably used more frequently, but as habits progress necessity is required more obsessively and possessively. As the pathological needs intensify, the conscience increasingly directs the strong demands for subconsciously formed obsessions, neurotic body movements, and body-image changes.

Obviously, life's miracle is not limited to the conscious, for all restrictions and studies must encompass the vastness of the subconscious. This, of course, both expands and complicates life; overall the subconscious programs the needs, and the conscience exerts the greater directions, and the resultant limitations are, often, somber indeed.

The general public, educators, therapists, and physicians frequently acknowledge ignorance and fear of the subconscious and conscience. Scholars largely ignore both while exploring the conscious, and their functions and controls are taught in high school biology classes as being autonomous. The author was criticized for introducing some bright high school students to their existences and functions.

Unfortunately, the subconscious, conscience functional directions are both positive and negative. The positive functions are very important because they include all the vital mental operations; they encompass memory and learning. Without both, there would never be any knowledge or accumulation of experience. Accordingly, the mind recalls memory, within certain emotional, personality-enforced limitations. Repressions, fear-reactions, utilized during traumas, whereby personalities force fears from the conscious, are also stored within the subconscious. Around those repressions, fears and anxieties are developed. Repetitious repressions frequently augment and timely intensify fears until they negatively limit and control personality development and severely restrict and shorten lives. The conscience (housed within the subconscious) possesses a subconsciously stored photographic memory; it becomes the storehouse of all life's events and the leading factor in personality developments. Ultimately, through repressive repetitions, all memory becomes more difficult, if not impossible, to precisely recall. The author thinks this is the leading cause of many low intelligent quotients, and the leading factor with the elderly as they exhibit difficulty in recalling previous events; frequently every personality is traumatized by similar events and utilizes almost identical adjustment methods with complete predictable results. If all stored memories were pleasant, life's problems would be mostly avoided.

To repress, individuals must encounter trauma. To encounter trauma, they usually interact within family drama and other significant situations. Those traumatic events (sometimes even trivial, except to the victims) are infrequently viewed calmly, but are experienced climactically; the events, through repressions, create subconscious fears, which are frequently exhibited by both youths and adults. Once fearful events are repressed, the pathological emotional adjustments become easier to use in almost identical situations, and anxieties (unexplained, strengthened fears) are formed and endured continually, which are further augmented with consequential-almost-identical repressions. As individuals age, the conscience becomes the personality protector; it's a shield from anxiety. Early in life, it's a child's companion, but through its mental and biological directions, it progressively programs emotional and ultimately physical changes, which are created to alleviate the raging anxiety; it often interferes with conscious-mature-emotional adjustments. Ultimately, the conscience simply employs other behavioral, pathological-adjustment mechanisms to hide the personality defects and accompanying anxiety; thereby, neurotic and psychotic personalities are born. Although the conscience is usually a friend during early personality developments, it frequently becomes an enemy during adulthood. The emotional intensification is more pronounced for highly neurotic and psychotic personalities because the conscience directs more rigid controls to shield higher anxieties, and those programmed emotional, pathological adjustments increasingly identify personalities and interfere with everyday living.

Many individuals then spend their lives hiding the fears, anxieties and the emotional and physical changes the conscience has programmed, which will be detailed in later chapters.

Since everyone has continually used repressions, the small voice (the conscience) increasingly demands more subconsciously born physical changes.

Conscious thoughts are originated and directed through many functions, mostly conscientiously. Daily decisions are never 100% negative or positive for well-adjusted personalities, but are frequently more negatively skewered for the more neurotic; they become more accentuated as individuals' age. For instance, well-adjusted personalities find it easier to control the emotion anger, but through aging and repetitious repressions, the more neurotic individuals find it more difficult. Anger is a consequence of repressions, and its byproduct is often hypertension, which helps program high blood pressure and diseases.

To calm the conscious, the subconscious must be treated. Then, if any long-range conscious changes are produced, all anxiety (subconsciously-induced anger augmentations) will automatically be reduced. Conversely, when fears are elevated, conscientiously controlled irregular body movements steadily, alarmingly increase, which is actuated because individuals through poor adjustments methods become increasingly intense and rigid; they automatically become more change resistant and more like themselves. Essentially, the conscientiously programmed directions strive to alleviate anxiety.

Within both fear repressions and pleasurable episodes, personalities are formed, but unfortunately individuals must spend many years living with the fears, which grow into anxieties. Even though the anxieties severely restrict life's choices, many individuals still reach sublime heights before declining and submitting to the programmed fates. For indeed, personalities are united with the sub-conscious and conscience, and the conscience is both a best friend and a strict guardian.

Chapter Two

The Subconscious Mind and You

The subconscious draws more negative opposition than almost any other topic. Although we live in the conscious, subconsciously formed fears and anxieties dominate all cognitions. The consequential emotional barriers, born within the subconscious, centered on the repressed fears, increasingly interfere with conscious thoughts and physical activity. Pathological emotional and physical habits become more common and increasingly difficult to hide. Negative adult decisions are emotionally intensified; positive decisions become more rare, especially with the psychotics and highly neurotics. Through aging, the conscience exerts more rigid controls; life becomes more self-stereotyped and emotionally predictable. Within the self-imposed strong, emotional, pathological, guidelines, restrictive life-styles are formed, which impose fewer positive choices; positive cognition and physical choices become difficult, if not impossible.

The consequentially increasing anxiety frequently orchestrates severely altered conscious body movements: involuntary hand or food movements, tremors, and muscular twitching.

Understandingly, the mind is compared to a television screen. The figures appearing on the screen are comparable to conscious thoughts, and everything causing the image-appearances is subconsciously and conscientiously programmed.

Obviously, the subconscious is more important than the conscious, as the conscious is merely the window to the subconscious. If doubts still remain, the author implores you to control your conscious thoughts extendedly. Remember, the subconscious stores fears and anxieties, and the conscience controls most conscious thoughts and behaviors. Overall, cognitions are 20 to 40% directed consciously, but the increased anxiety levels demand stronger conscience directives. Therefore when anger, a subconsciously formed fear byproduct, is partially controlled through conscious efforts only, it will increasingly interfere with cognition. Questionably, counselors advocate conscious regulation of anger and thereby program many future emotional and physical problems because well-adjusted individuals live with anger easily, but highly neurotic and psychotic individuals pay a terrible price: cardiovascular problems, physical violence towards others, incarcerations, and death.

To change pathological conscious behavior, the subconscious must be treated, and if well-adjusted emotional conscious change is sought, the conscientiously induced strong emotions must be reduced.

Unfortunately, conscientiously directed personality formations are programmed through many factors: both pleasant and unpleasant episodes. The traumas, which precipitate repressions, causing anxieties, which increases with aging, are accepted as a normal happenstance.

For the poet is accurate, "I have met the enemy and he is I." Although the subconscious and conscious form an integral unit, they are not equal. There is however interplay between them, especially within the surface areas, as memory from the subconscious programs cognitions. Strong emotions hinder the process, which is exhibited with highly neurotic, psychotic, and elderly individuals, who frequently suffer memory problems.

Repetitious repressions and aging promote highly neurotic and psychotic personalities. Aging and repressions also help orchestrate elderly pathological behaviors and deaths. With both, the conscience, a vital mind part, ceases to act as a friend and becomes an enemy. Unfortunately, reality distortions and pathological body changes (images) follow. Although the facts are dire, they aren't unchangeable. Read on.

Obviously, the emotionally mature personalities have more personal choice options; the conscience exerts fewer limitations, but the more emotionally immature ones lose positive personal choices through strong emotions, and they simply over-react to more outside trauma. The more mature are serene while the maladjusted are intense because the conscience erects emotional barriers centered on repressed fears to alleviate anxiety; those anxiety levels create emotionally self-perceived weakness to which maladjusted individuals must over-react. The manufactured fears (housed, produced, subconsciously) increase emotional and physical failures while decreasing successes. Personalities, thereby, become self-deceptive as they increasingly blame others for their self-imposed limitations.

Consequently the fears and anxieties are always produced through consciously encountered trauma and are never centered on performed conscious acts. The repressed fears and the consequently formed anxieties are factually produced by what sufferers fear they will do, and they repress the unthinkable thoughts. The traumatized, pathological responses and the restrictive self-imposed limitations, unfortunately, now remain within the subconscious and must be lived with; neurotic personalities have simply grown more like themselves, and the conscience has become the enemy.

The subconscious has not only become the storehouse of knowledge, but even more importantly, it has become the platform for all cognitions and behaviors. Exhibited consciously, but drawn from the subconscious; fears, anxieties, and subsequent anger dominate cognitions. Deep within the subconscious are harbored ominous

and threatening anxieties that alter cognitive activities severely limit choices, and shorten lives.

The conscience has many other functions that are very important: it directs all heart activity, various glandular secretions, estab-
lishes the metabolic rate, and controls the blood pressure, the im-
mune- systems actions, the digestive tract abilities, and every physically important body function. The subconscious houses the personality, and the conscience, somewhat, forms, limits, and protects
it; every physical function that is not totally consciously controlled
is completely or partly directed conscientiously. The medical profession has mislabeled them as, autonomous functions (whatever
that means).

Then personalities are captains of their bodies; but unfortunately, not completely through cognitions or rational logic, but most
frequently by and through subconsciously repressed fears and anxieties.

Yet, the conscious directs many body activities somewhat, but
the subconscious and conscience commands and overrides most
body functions and uses because of anxieties and fears. Illustrative-
ly, tremors consequently follow traumas and alcohol debauchery,
and stress often interferes with sleep and other activities; many are
unwelcome consciously. Through those and many other dire consequences, the conscience overrides cognitive efforts. The conscience
exertions, programmed to protect the personality, frequently, distort cognition and direct distorted body movements that can completely disrupt and stop vital body functions.

Through fears and anxieties, the conscience helps form personalities; for instance, the subconscious stores the reasons for individuals' idiosyncrasies. The warehoused repressions help form individualities, and ultimately, they also largely compute productive
and nonproductive days. Within the subconscious, directed by the
conscience, individuals' lives, destiny and most frequently deaths
are programmed. All will be detailed in later chapters.

Men and women insist on and thrive with individuality; the price, however, is frequently horrific, for the repressions, which helped form the personalities, progressively intensify and become the directing factor in vocations, mate selections, forced and chosen life-styles and ultimately the type, time, and procedure of death.

Every one seemingly believes that each day is different and new events await; frequently those assumptions are not factual, for life is viewed and endured through the same imperfect, flawed personalities. Thereby, each day individuals encounter near identical events and employ the same adjustments techniques, and their cognitive choices are increasingly restricted through the strengthened emotions. Therefore, their idiosyncrasies are intensified and anxieties are increased. They've simply become more like themselves, and future options have been more restricted. Within the more rigid personalities, individuals distrust themselves, and they view the future alarmingly.

Progressively, traumas and repressions consequently program fears; they intensify and consequently compute anxieties; and they consequently, compulsively require the building of emotional barriers, formed to protect personalities.

Personalities are orchestrated partly by trauma interactions; but are also produced by parental interactions, and loved and admired ones' emulations.

Unfortunately, repressed fears, dreads, and anxieties repetitiously resurface; consequently, with the increased tension, the conscience must react to stronger emotions. Tragic results are often inevitable. While the emotional causes are partly hidden by the repressions, the effects are carried for a lifetime. The author once had a dear lady say: "some things are best left within the subconscious." If leaving them there, they become dormant or psychologically expunged, she and the author would have been in accord. But that is never the case, because around those fears, dreads, and anxieties, personalities change personal images, established life-styles, and build lives. The dire changes come slowly, but comprehensively. Most individuals, scientists and medical doctors confuse psychological changes with aging. However, the personal, emotional and psychological mal-adaptations are never normal aging, as the conscience must erect additional abnormal emotional and physical barriers to contain the increasing anxieties. These and other dangerous adaptations will be discussed along with the terrible price they exact, in the following chapters.

The fore mentioned psychological and biological changes are not neurosis, but are programmed by strong neurotic formations and become conscious exhibitions, which become personality incorporations and dominate individuals. Lives are spent pursuing the psychologically demanded abnormalities. The more severely threatened personalities must live their lives in the extremely restricted, chosen, and limiting life-styles.

The subconscious is a mind part; the conscience, enclosed within it, is also a moral guide and ethical voice, and its functions direct all biological and emotional equilibrium, which is somewhat dependent on emotionally, pathologically erected life-styles and physical barriers that demand tremendous sacrifices.

Personalities easily and obviously exhibit the increasingly compelled changes: physical, habitual, and emotional, which are required because as emotional traumas are encountered, repetitiously, bodies conscientiously adopt. Adrenaline, conscientiously programmed, inters the bloodstream. Heart activity increases and blood pressure elevates. The lungs produce more oxygen to the blood; all are emergency survival activities. Through the process, personalities run faster or fight harder. Unfortunately, the development has also become pathological; with anxiety, everyone frequently, continually programs similar biological and psychological adaptations. All anxiety, including the elevated, is always pathological, as it exhibits conscientiously enforced fears consciously. The extreme biological examples are then psychologically demanded and experienced consciously. The negative-stressful process is viewed in ulcer, heart, and kidney patients: the stress is not the minor part that many professionals (including doctors) express, but is the inner unrest programmed by many repressions, exhibited through uncontrolled body shakes; it orchestrates illnesses, and diseases.

This writing is also aimed at individuals' morals that are taught to the young, which serve a vital part within younger children, but it's aimed mostly toward those same morals that play a disruptive function with the more maladjusted individuals. It's found deeply imbedded within their intensive personalities. Obviously, good moral behavior is always associated with adjusted personalities, and poor moral behavior is frequently associated with the maladjusted. Poor moral adjustments are always augmented through repetitious repressions, and are always psychologically reinforced. Additionally, through aging, personalities grow more intense; the increased tension is frequently centered on personal morals. The self-destructive defense mechanisms, employed during stress, augment the problems; resisting the strong urges help form and re-enforce a vicious cycle. Frequently, a flight into enforced life-styles is a result. Obesity, an anxiety-avoidance technique, could be an obvious example. Over eating and the consequential weight gain frequently programs complacency. Although the weight gain is usually not in their best interest, personalities frequently, somewhat, relax but become complacent; they have not broken any moral values. They have simply surrendered to strong conscientiously orchestrated urges and retreated within themselves. If the weight gain is somewhat limited, society mostly ignores it. The victims have fled to a life-style that is terribly limiting, possessive, and frequently deadly. Unfortunately, all life-styles are exactly that. They will be more detailed in following chapters.

Strong emotions are always pathological and subconsciously formed by repressions; viewed consciously, they're windows into the subconscious. Emotional and physical barriers (reprehensibly and comprehensibly programmed to shield personalities from life threatening anxiety) are completely illogical; yet they dominate conscious living.

The emotional barriers then program another name, neurosis. Personalities exhibit subconsciously formed, conscientiously induced strong emotions, consciously; they're called neurosis, which is a common term equated to imperfect personalities. The individual neurotic differences are found in the emotional strengths and repressions within personalities. The greater emotional strengths demand stronger conscientiously enforced conscious exhibitions, which also increase tensions. The greater tensions demand stronger conscious controlling efforts. But unfortunately the fears that enforce the conscious non-compliance behaviors are always pathological.

The fears, anxieties, and psychologically adaptive behaviors then become life-threatening issues, as life-styles and physical-adoptive methods quickly follow. Disease and deaths are then programmed. The life-styles and physical adaptations can also be called symptoms of neurosis and are always pathologically induced.

The threatened conscience dictates limited and restricted conscious behaviors. The neurotically strong personalities, centered on those strong emotions, are attracted to rigidly controlled, behavioral life-styles. Although the restrictive limitations are always self-imposed, they, somewhat allay anxiety. But, the life-styles' barriers and boundaries are seldom sufficient, for augmented anxieties demand extreme-limitations, which further restrict conscious options. Personalities, then, are forced to adapt to other life-styles for further anxiety reductions, which the conscience sets the limits, boundaries, and needs. The restraints and restrictions come from two sources: They automatically exist with the personality-compelled physical changes, and they are re-enforced within the life-styles themselves. Centered on the repressed fears, both the body-changes and life-style adaptations are programmed to simply reduce or control ragging anxieties. Since the life-styles' characteristics and programmed physical-restraints are compulsively and compelling sought, the more intense comfort seeker will find only partial relief, which is consistent with individual needs, and those are constantly changing with individualistic anxiety levels.

Many life-styles are frequently seen and have become so common that they're mostly ignored. The more common ones, which dominate personalities, are viewed in almost every society and are shared in every vocation and profession.

The more prominent are the following: The severely obese and the extremely pro-sexist male or female are frequently found and often encouraged in both the families and in societies. The homosexual male and female and the athletic male and female are frequently seen, and another is the greatly accentuated academic people of either sex. The more obvious is the deeply religious personalities, who by their dress and customs are easily identified. The strongly identified peaceful dove types of either sex are still found. Consistent drug users, including alcohol, form their own groups, and are seen in most of the other life-styles. Also, both criminal and crime control people form their own separations, but also adapt to other limiting life-styles to allay anxiety. The list also includes the reclusive and semi-reclusive people who adopt cultural changes and flee from their inner fears. The list, of course, is not conclusive, but merely introduces the topic of life-styles. Highly neurotic personalities must seek several adaptations simultaneously to dampen ragging anxieties.

For instance, the pro-sexual individuals, of either sex, compellingly exhibit their dreaded fears in various selected adaptations. The early youth formations are obviously formatted around anger, rage, and anxiety. Self-doubt and inferiority complexes are easily seen, and the personalities are frequently attracted to excessive body building adventures. Their friend-selection and clothing are easily identifiable; the clothing frequently centers on anti-scholastic selections. The troubled-scholastic nonconformities, frequently compellingly, program the young adults to vocations and away from formal education. Through their anxieties, they now proudly show their abnormal pro-sexual characteristics. Within the lifestyles and group participation, the pathologically chosen clothing, hairstyles, and other mannerisms easily re-enforce the stereotype. Auto purchases are also mostly pre-required: they're either a fast sport car or a flashy pick-up truck. The group characteristics are repressively nurtured, housed, and required through personalities that are developed with and centered on their repressions.

Unfortunately, those individuals must utilize the same pro-sexual thinking in matrimonial selections. The stereotyped mental process will be strongly, sexually influenced. Their troubled marriages produce highly neurotic children who are raised in authoritative family atmospheres. The pro-sexual males usually make poor husbands and fathers. Deep anxieties, frequently exhibited within the families, program alcohol and other drug use. Scotch and beer match their pro-sexual thinking. Frequently, the males and females are found in bars, involved in altercations, with other patrons, centered on sex, sports, and other stereotyped behavioral topics.

Traffic courts, compellingly programmed with neurotic impatience and fast driving, are required; incarcerations are frequent. Being accident prone, they carry the questionable attribute through out life.

Anti-authoritative personalities, consciously exhibiting anger, frequently develop allergies, arthritis, asthmatic attacks, and common colds. As the midyears approach, life-threatening images (physical changes) are formed to allay anxiety. Fat accumulates around the waistlines. Hypertension, cardiovascular problems, and malignant-growths become common. Rigid personalities, and stereotype-thought patterns necessitate many anxiety-decreasing psychological-defense-methods; any disease, consequently follow-ing, which is pathologically demanded, will increasingly be life threatening.

Unfortunately, the author has seen the previous example many times. Obviously, fear repressions and individual thought patterns program many personality variables. Blended with the varied per-sonalities, the conscience commands conscious thoughts and ac-tions that dominate lives; they're largely and frighteningly limited by the repressions, their repetitions, and anxiety's degree of inten-sity.

Living within the life-styles and exhibiting strong, rigid, person-ality patterns, personalities are then accurately called, "neurotic." Our interest must now center on those strong neurotic patterns.

Chapter Three

The Subconscious Mind and Neurosis

The author is aware that this is a disquieting subject because of viewing oneself neurotically is very disturbing; living within, and limited by, the timely honed, but poorly adjusted personalities, individuals become accustomed to personal thought patterns, even though the cognitions are centered on pathological events. Neurosis, according to Webster's Dictionary is, "suffering from emotional instability." The opposite to that is emotional perfection, a worthy wish but not a realistic expectation.

Universally, everyone adopts an emotion called, anger; it's a pathological defense mechanism, or an emotional response. Although it's completely and harmfully pathological, it's harbored and developed throughout every life. It's either consciously displayed, when emotionally or physically threatened, or subconsciously repressed; the latter requires a lifetime of denial. Although it's always adopted while personalities are young and is intensified throughout life, it simply shields personalities from anxiety. It's generally personalized during frustrating traumas, which programs frequent repressions. Through its employment, individuals figuratively regress emotionally; it's a shield form strong traumatic emotional or physical confrontations, but prevents mature emotional adjustments. The traumatically emotional, progressed adjustments are pathological, and understandably are poorly and timely employ-able. For instance, the author knows a man who is five foot, five inches tall who has developed masculine-sexuality doubts. When addressed with short statue issues, he will always respond with angry personal-sexual-prowess contentions. Manhood, to him, is equivalent to physical size and sexual prowess. Seemingly; everyone, everywhere, is psychologically, possessively driven to prove sexuality. This sheer madness portrays itself throughout every society as it transverses social barriers. Frequently lives are ruined, when simply seeking emotional help would be a realistic solution. Obviously, neurosis is universal; personally accepting the label is difficult. Personalities have lived within their bodies and minds since birth and have grown accustomed to individual thought patterns, resultant behaviors, and subsequent results. Even though the results are highly neurotic, poorly reasoned, frequently centered on fear and anxiety, and program abnormal human trauma, they're progressively retained in pathologically directed lives. Well-adjusted psychological change is never an option. Within the emotionally restrictive, extremely limited lives, demons and tigers are mentally personalized; they dominate cognitions and behaviors; time is, then spent disproving the self-created compulsions. And as obsessions intensify, behaviors become more neurotic and personalities become more rigid. Personalities have simply become more like themselves.

The question is asked: how and why do personalities become neurotic and adopt negative changes that limit and frequently shorten lives? Simple, the subconscious stores fears; the conscience reacts to alleviate the programmed, consequential anxieties, and through the subconscious fears and augmentations, ultimately, neurotic behavior is required. Repressions consequently form fears and anxieties; they, thereby, dominate, limit, shorten, and destroy lives. Factually, fears and anxieties become the lives.

Unfortunately, the fearful repressions are never fully, subconsciously expunged because the conscience deals in black and white issues, only. When emotional issues are repressed, an accusing conscience views the personality guiltily; there are no shades of gray.

As those fearful repressions are repeated through almost identical traumas, individuals become more neurotic, and consciences must increase the emotional barriers to protect the fragile and neurotic personalities. Days are simply lived identically as the day before, completely dominated by fears and anxieties. As anxieties always intensify, emotional barriers consequently are increased, and greater effort is demanded to calm the ragging emotional intensities. Those calming efforts are frequently centered on self-denials and non-compliances because time is spend showing the world that the emotional issues don't exist.

As anxieties increase, personalities become unable to work, sleep, or play properly, and frequently have reoccurring nightmares centered on subconsciously formed anxieties because the conscience is trying to enlighten and heal the conscious. The nightmares' central theme is always revealing, except to the sufferer.

An obese couple, the author once knew, had reoccurring nightmares of food shortages that dominated their sleep; food and its procurement dominated their conversation and lives, and they carried excessive food with them while traveling, stored food in their desks, and hid their heads wile excessively eating. Food dominated their thought process and became their lives. Although it was obviously an extreme obsession, it was still only a byproduct. Centered upon repressions, it was programmed by excessive eating, that the conscience used to shield the couple, from a ragging anxiety. To protect the fragile personalities, the conscience simply increased the compulsion, and the emotional and physical barriers were increased to strengthen a physical or emotional noncompliance. They identified their adopted life-style. The subconsciously stored the repressions, and repetitious traumas helped reinforce the neuroses; their personalities simply developed more like themselves.

Unfortunately, idiosyncrasies are formed, and personalities become different. Through those fears, individualities are formed and proudly displayed, while denying the existences, and groups are joined with identical behavior patterns. The adopted life-styles then exact multiple penalties, which are demanded daily and since the emotional problems become physical, the penalties multiply. As personalities are partly formed by repressed fears, idiosyncrasies are programmed to reduce the consequential anxiety. Individuals thereby carry the problems throughout their lives; they frequently flee from themselves, and the self-imposed emotional fleeing is portrayed physically by conscientiously controlled foot movements, hand shaking, and muscular jerking.

Unfortunately, the physical and intense emotional changes demand costs that require a lifetime to pay because the physical changes (image changes) simply restrict the personality, but somewhat insure physical non-compliances; the developed idiosyncrasies display the neurosis, orchestrate consequentially required image changes, and thereby induce and enforce life-styles adaptations.

The subconsciously stored emotions and the conscience dominate the conscious, as the latter almost completely reflects the compulsions. Through traumas, the conscience, bedded within the subconscious, becomes the moral and ethical agent. If personalities were born emotionally and physically mature, the conscience would be less important. But while young, personalities repress fears, which help form personality patterns, which remain with the individuals throughout their lives. Unfortunately the consequential patterns and habits are intensified by additional repressions, and the conscience, then, becomes more controlling. Conscientiously erected emotional barriers frequently program physical changes and require the selection and adoption of life-styles. Through those self-erected barriers, created by fears and anxieties, personalities develop inferiority complexes. When traumas encourage repressions, the conscience judges in black or white guilt issues only. When fears are harbored within the subconscious, personalities are guiltily self-judged; multiple repressed fears consequentially produce pathologically strong inferiority complexes because through those fears and anxieties, personally perceived self-evaluations are lowered. The strongly developed inferiority complexes are menacing, unwelcome guests that increasingly demand dire costs.

They are emotional conditions usually formed by the young, and unfortunately, children and adults struggle with many conscious fears centered on the emotional developments. Frequently, both groups react to the consequential anxiety by committing suicide. Others develop superiority complexes to hide the ragging anxieties. Throughout life, individuals, simply, cover their flawed personalities with partial successes and failures. Adolph Hitler, born in Austria, 1889, died in Germany in 1945, psychotically adopted a superiority complex to hide an inferiority complex and allay a ragging anxiety. The developed idiosyncrasies program strong emotional barriers, consequential image-changes, life-style adaptations, and many illnesses. The costs are staggering, and the developments are almost impossible to recognize by the sufferers themselves.

Increasingly, the complexes force the conscience to create failure fears, calamity fears, anxiety attacks, dreadful disease fears, and repetitious nightmares. Simply the personalities and the consequential costs grow, dominate lives, and become the resultant lives; they increasingly require greater effort to hide the effects, and the emotional barriers are necessarily increased.

Having an inferiority complex is not terribly important, because everyone has one somewhat, but the strength and the emotional and physical cost are very important. Since having one and being neurotic are commonly shared, complacency and total ignorance become deadly. The increasingly consequential emotional burdens are the following: nervous irritability, increased anger, intense fear and anxiety, self-esteem loss, self-respect and cognitive-ability decrease, emotional-adjustment-ability loss, and premature death. Unfortunately, the repressed fears (which program inferiority complexes) were relevant to childhood and totally irrelevant to adulthood. But the emotional barriers and adopted life-styles, enact terrible required costs.

Following repressions, personalities pathologically select behavioral characteristics and conscientiously demanded adjustment techniques or mechanisms that are used as anxiety avoidances; they are completely neurotic.

They, in fact, eventually augment additional emotional maladjustments. Frustration and anxiety form poor partnerships and lead to physical and emotional disasters.

Each selected adjustment technique always follows pathological repressions. They are the following: projection, rationalization, denial, distortion, sour grapes, over-compensation, over-identification, reaction formation, dissociation, and substitution. As the defense mechanisms are personalized their future utilizations are established. Unfortunately, the compelling employments are necessitated by the increasing anxieties; combined, they and the conscience form vicious cycles. They're created with the consuming guilt that is felt and partly hidden, and the selected mechanism that increases anxiety, simply, reveal rather than hide the emotional problems.

Repression, a frequently used mechanism, is well recognized, but universally ignored, and its destructive nature shortens, restricts and bemeans lives; it always precedes all other defense usages.

When individual-personality-traits are viewed threateningly, personalities, simply employ the projection defense mechanism; thereby the troublesome neurosis is transferred to others, and briefly, the neurotic become less anxious; future use is always demanded. It's seen with paranoids who are increasingly threatened by their repressed-killing fears, usually centered on their parents, and they simply, mentally project the repressed fear to others, which, somewhat relieves the projector. Unfortunately, tragedy is consequently, frequently programmed, for highly neurotic individuals kill mentally imagined or real enemies.

Rationalization is used when justification is compellingly necessitated to assuage some behavioral or emotional need or acquisition. Although completely pathological, its employment temporarily alleviates anxiety. The author once worked with a group of people who were going broke financially, but continually bought new and expensive cars, because they deserved them.

Burdened with unacceptable personality traits, programmed through obvious inferiority complexes, while visibly showing all the characteristics, the existences are simply denied. Some patients with terminal diseases exhibit a total indifference.

Through distortion, the significances are decreased or increased; consciences, simply, distort the events to blend with the emotional needs.

Bipolar personalities distort present circumstances to blend with their emotional moods; from within less than perfect personalities, they simply perceive themselves as perfect or severally damaged. Dangerously, it increases anxiety and reduces any inner urge for help.

Sour grapes are used if individuals fail in some endeavor and assert they would not have wanted it, if obtained; the un-obtained grapes were sour.

Compensation or over-compensation is used if personalities distort emotional maladjustments. Just as the short acquaintance over-compensated for his limited statue by constantly referring to his sexual prowess, others hide self-perceived problems through elevated emotionality's. Responding angrily, upon being confronted, they somewhat are compensating for some self-perceived emotional or physical problem; they are pathologically over-reacting, but are normally neurotic.

Personalities, who exhibit excessive or deviate sexual appetites, are simply overcompensating from subconsciously born sexual insecurities; the nation and the entire world's population are mostly, conscientiously, sexually overreacting. Enlarged food appetites, although pathological and dangerous, are somewhat different; they too are overcompensations. Created within the subconscious and exhibited consciously, they are partly fueled through deflated egos, which program vicious cycles, and necessitate further overreactions. Unfortunately, societies help program the vicious cycle by advertising food rewards while using sexually attractive attendants. Both the food and sex overcompensations are pathological and common, but neurotic.

Personalities who harbor perceived unacceptable personality traits, frequently employ reaction formation acts; they simply exhibit the opposite. Some mothers, fearing strong, poor parenting skills, join various programs to prove their superiority. Many severely over-weight individuals, (hiding a ragging, repressed anger), transform the subconscious need and show a gentle nature. Frequently, individuals who perform some behavior in sequence with another illogical, pathological behavior are also using reaction-formation acts.

Disassociation is a much used adjustment method. It's used when personalities visualize emotional or physical problems negatively; they simply disassociate the trait. Hysterics use it to shield themselves from elevated anxieties; multiple personalities are subconsciously necessitated by strong anxieties centered on conscience judging of moral and ethical values. Strong anxieties require the personality splitting to separate a morally split personality from one that must be immorally isolated. Accordingly, personalities develop many emotional problems and alleviate anxiety by disassociation. Habits are adopted that shield them from anxiety; the compulsions are called compulsive-disassociate behaviors.

Conscientiously controlled hand or foot movements are easily categorized; they are demanded to mask and to alleviate anxieties centered on repressed fears. The author saw his and other individuals' involuntary hand and foot movements disappear following therapy that removed repressions involving parental to childhood corporal punishment.

In summary, repression is, by far, the most harmful defensive mechanism. It's the first and most destructive mechanism employed, and it's always found when neurosis is treated; a few prenatal embryos have shown pathological signs of its employment. Its use programs other harmful defensive's usage.

Every defense-mechanism-utilization is an anxiety-adjusting behavior, and it's emotionally, repressively required; future employment instantly disappear, following the transfer of repressed memories from the subconscious to the conscious.

Juveniles frequently repress fears, which progressively form anxieties; unfortunately, adults don't have, without therapy, the ability to recall traumatically repressed events. The neurotic repression, and the accompanying fear and anxiety, require conscious emotional distancing; conscious fears promote-almost require-continual, nearly identical repressions; thereby anxieties are created, and intensified.

Around traumas, repressed events, and the consequential programmed neuroses, lives are formed. As the pathological, emotional needs increase, anxieties are strengthened, and strong emotional and physical barriers are protectively erected. Time is then spent to prove to the world that the neuroses don't exist. Unfortunately, the time and effort are never successful because the subconsciously developed inferiority complexes intensify. Developed pathological thoughts surface consciously, continually; living with them will eventually exact grim results. Obviously, the word neurotic can be enlarged to include everyone, because personalities universally harbor fears and anxieties, and eventually die from the consequentially related causes.

But, what is anxiety? It's an augmented fear that has no discernable conscious cause, which has been intensified through time and repetitious repressions. Although its causes are not consciously exhibited, the symptoms and consequential-behaviors are always displayed; some sufferers frequently live through periodical anxiety attacks. Unfortunately, individuals experience traumas and repress the fears with varying personalities; almost identical traumatic experiences will activate the same repressive rationale, with different, personally required behaviors.

Experiencing anxieties, many and varied avoidance mechanisms that are programmed through strong neurotic growths must be compellingly utilized. The emotional stresses program many different emotional behaviors and orchestrate various physical changes. They, anxiety-reduction induced, timely increase and augment anxiety levels. Conscientiously programmed physical changes and physical movements are as varied as the personalities who compellingly employ them: any physical movement that is not completely consciously controlled is, in part, or totally conscientiously controlled. Accordingly, as stress increases, the conscientiously programmed involuntary movements will increase. The symptoms become more significant because they reappear in illness symptoms and death causes.

All biological symptoms are partially conscientiously controlled. Stored repressions program fears and anxieties, which in turn, promote insecure feelings, inferiority complexes, defense mechanism usages, and life-style limitations. Within the subconscious, neurotic behaviors originate, intensify, and if left untreated, dominate the personality. Unfortunately, in time they not only limit lives but also frequently, prematurely end them.

There are many individual stressful signs. Some personalities develop work habit problems; jobs are over accentuated. Successes are over evaluated, while others shun the successful chances. The latter group program failures. Accordingly, it's obvious that personalities, who commit suicide when confronted with failure, have indeed overemphasized success. Their inferiority complexes that program deep insecure feelings prevent living with failures. Some personalities fear that they will personally perform violent acts on others; they withdraw and become recluses or hermits, while reacting to the same psychological needs, somewhat, but show different behavioral characteristics.

Commonly, there are many ways to camouflage inferiority complexes; some anxiety reducing methods are the following: all non-medical drug use (including alcohol), some prescribed drug use, all neurotic behavior, all psychotic behavior, all criminal behavior, and all anti-social behavior are included. Simply, personalities are neurotic because individuals live with unresolved emotional issues centered on repressed fears. Anxiety-avoidance techniques, pathologically shielding mechanisms, are adopted through conscientious programming. Through them lives are restricted, distorted, and shortened. Alarmingly, when neuroses grow (with anxiety intensifications), they frequently program psychoneuroses and psychoses, for instance, senility, or Alzheimer disease.

Indeed, neurosis is common; just as inferior complexes are equally endured; both are denied and hidden, but the futile efforts are never successful because both of them compellingly program conscious behaviors that defy reality. If the pathological-maladjustment causes were consciously formed, rather than subconsciously, the shameful denial would be more curably easy. The deceitful, insidious hiding is never flattering or healthy and with time becomes deadly. Exhibited sexual deviations, conscientiously directed to alleviate anxiety, are glaringly and proudly displayed even though the subject includes much emotional trauma; it, too, is a subconsciously stored, conscientiously controlled behavior, programmed through and with repressions.

Food and sex excesses are recognizably easy; problematically viewing them is extremely difficult, and many personalities exhibit both extremes. Both neurotic exhibitions have been here throughout time; the Romans used them. Provably, food and sex excesses were then, and are now, pathological and common; the consequential exhibitions haven't varied. Unfortunately, the extreme food and sex usages are more prevalent with affluent societies, and when combined with extended leisure time, they help program neurotic behavior displays; the grim consequential results have increased.

Through enlarging and increasing emotional problems, and intensifying inferiority complexes, mature adjustment abilities decrease.

Employed, the related defense mechanisms (a pathological by-product) are socially, negatively viewed, but they frequently are proudly exhibited. The victims, employing the neurotically adopted physical and behavior changes, are striving to prove that the original fearful repressions are not personally housed.

Reclusive individuals adopt antisocial personal behavior and seek isolation, while others adopt varied and different life-styles to alleviate increasing anxieties. Social climbers frequently use social position to disprove and hide inferiority feelings. Strong complexes, fearfully induced, frequently compel heroic action. All adopted life-styles limit, restrict, and regulate life. The adopted emotional barriers program pathological, consequential conscious actions and overreactions. However, as long as the victims remain within the limiting structures, stress is lessened, but unfortunately only briefly.

Just as obese individuals overeat and consequently gain additional weight, other life-style seekers also react to conscientiously chosen fears and anxieties, and thereby increase their obsessive behaviors, and severally restrict consequently dominated physical, sexual, and economic lives. Yet even with the life-styles' staggering costs, personalities adopt them and remain faithful, after becoming convinced that the decisions were indeed pathological. Obviously, many personalities must know that their personal stress is abnormal; perhaps it's another denial form, and it simply aids cognitive emotional barrier building and enhances life-style conformity.

Chapter Four

The Subconscious Mind and Physical Changes

The subconscious has an unlimited capacity of storing repressions; the consciences has an unrelenting role of protecting the personality; frequently, combined, they program biological changes that are consequently dire. Indeed, orchestrated body changes are directed through strong neurotic emotions, which are pathologically, obsessively demanded to alleviate anxiety. Being deeply, subconsciously induced, and conscientiously, compellingly directed, personalities frequently develop severe changes with the more intense central emotional issues. Repeatedly, emotional and physical barriers are programmed subconsciously, directed conscientiously and exhibited consciously; all are timely compellingly, and emotionally intensified. The conscience has simply placed an additional controlling barrier to shield the personality from self-induced anxieties.

After negative fears are repressed, as closely related traumatic events are experienced, emotional barriers are erected that are centered on the fears and anxieties. When they no longer dispel the anxieties, additional physical barriers, centered on the original repressions, are compellingly erected. Those physical changes are always compellingly displayed and place another barrier between the victims and their fears. With the physical alterations, personalities become, somewhat, more relaxed, but they also become more complacent and resist healthy therapeutic interventions.

The author studied a case in which a mother used corporal punishment in the home. She was dictatorial and strongly opposed the teenage son's emotional reactions. The son consequentially repressed many, strong fears of chocking his mother, and soon his life was dominated. After some time and emotional trauma had elapsed, rheumatoid arthritis twisted his hands, and they gradually lost some function. The consequential hand deformity simply placed a physical barrier between the teenager and the dreaded fears, which also produced a grotesque and limiting life-style; the arthritis reduced or allayed the anxiety, but additional repressions require increased pathological arthritic developments.

The psychological and physical changes that the conscience can program are almost unnumbered because personalities are living longer, and more and varied ways are orchestrated to shield anxiety. The following are the more obvious; obesity, emaciation, stooped shoulders, any poor posture, clumsy gate, homosexuality, over sexuality, under sexuality, all non-heterosexuality, most physically crippling, any body disfigurement, baldness or any exaggerated hair loss, most, if not all illnesses, and perhaps most deaths.

As repressed fears intensify, the fears become anxieties, which consequentially program strong emotionally limiting barriers and frequently physical changes, which are often crippling. In turn, life-styles are formed; consciences have placed additional barriers between sufferers and their anxieties.

Enlarged nutritional appetites, almost completely conscientiously controlled, promote obvious prearranged limitations of life. Repressed fears program angry personalities and frequently require enlarged appetites, which usually produce obesity; it simply becomes the physical barrier between the personality and the increasing anxiety. Obesity's limiting qualities are vast and dire: sufferers become less mobile, socially unacceptable, somewhat sexually unattractive, employment choices are restricted, and lives are also shortened; the conscience's aim, centered around the original repressions, is frequently found in the varied results. Obviously the conscience alters lives, both physically and emotionally, and partly insures non-participation from repressed fears, which are both consciously unpleasant and unwanted. The changes are gradual and are consciously accepted through their inclining dominance: their limitations, restrictions; and life threatening attributes naturally produce conscious life-style thoughts. The sufferers simply state they don't have a problem they only like what they do; so entire personalities are engrossed within the fearful ideation. They have simply grown more like themselves.

The recluse's life-style is a perfect example because, as those personalities fear social contact, they increasingly avoid public confrontations and eventually seek complete physical and emotional seclusion. The increasing fears quicken the physical withdrawal; their consciences program conscious thoughts, which necessitates seclusion. Within its physical restrictions, they will be somewhat safer from their repressed anxieties. The life-styles also program other related issues to insure fearful non-compliances. Frequently, recluses adopt poor hygienic habits, poor dressing, and un-kept hair, which additionally ensure limited social contacts. The habit-needs (both within the subconscious, conscientiously enacted, expressed consciously through desires) simply, partly assure individuals that they will not fulfill their fears.

Sexual deviation, another anxiety avoidance, non-participation, psychological adaptation, is also programmed by repressed fears. It isn't physical but promotes changes that are both psychological and biological. The behavioral changes are usually psychologically programmed while the sufferers are very young, and are always centered on repressed sexual fears.

Sexual deviation includes all sexual changes, which deviate from heterosexuality; all are conscientiously programmed to alleviate anxiety. The sexual perversities serve as barriers, centered on strong emotions, which produce limiting life-styles and severely altered lives.

Oversexed personalities (a world majority) also program and divert sexual thought patterns centered on pathologically born repressions. Unfortunately, the near identical subconsciously born, conscientiously directed needs or desires compute all pathologically conceived different and bizarre sexual extremes. The maladjustments and the original repressions' participants (frequently both the perpetrators and the victims' personalities) produce the abnormal and often illegal behaviors. Living within highly neurotic personalities, which over-empathize the extremes, individuals psychologically, provably display sexually oriented thoughts that distort logic. The deviated changes, including increased and decreased desires, originated with the strongly repressed fears. The driven personalities (utilizing pathological abnormalities) distant themselves from the repression-born anxieties; they try to prove, somewhat, that the anxieties never existed. Unfortunately, the sexual deviations and the accompanying strong emotional barriers are viciously interwoven, and the formed inferiority complexes produce strong guilt thoughts and patterns; the conscience simply, complexly alters the needs, and tries to alleviate anxieties centered on the subconsciously stored repressions.

Although sexual pervasions are not completely physical, they frequently help incorporate physical changes: homosexual personalities, through conscientiously altered strong, pathological desires, frequently, change their bodies and sexual images. The physically altered images simple endeavor to further distance them from the original repressed fears and anxieties. Some, through progressive anxiety, endure surgical operations that physically display their mentally programmed neurotic life-styles.

Factually, no one is entirely heterosexual or homosexual; complex personalities simply harbor male and female characteristics.

Obviously, children are acquainted with both adult male and female figures.

Anorexia (a subconsciously formed, conscientiously induced nutritional need disorder) programs physical changes. Individuals (mostly women, through inadequate calorie ingestions) simply alter images to meet emotional and physical needs. The consequently demanded alterations obviously mirror the conscientiously controlled sexual demands.

Other pathological physical changes, the conscience programs are less obvious, but just as insidious. Hair loss, for instance, is widely considered an inherited characteristic, yet hair growth, too, is controlled within the subconscious. Anxiety, inner tension, alters and interferes with the normal hair balance control. The conscience simply alters hair retention to buffer anxiety. Time and increased tension programs additional hair loss. All emotionally motivated physical alterations must increase as anxieties augment, as the continual physical exaggerations will always equal the anxiety degrees.

The pathologically chosen life-styles will never serve personalities well. Essentially, they (helping to create the limiting, destroying, and controlling environments, which have programmed the vicious cycles) will program deaths. Prior to death, as the pathologically repressed fears intensity, personalities must endure more preselected emotional, physical, and sexual extremes.

Living within a continually restricting and demanding life-style, emotionally threatened personalities are virtually dominated. Therefore individuals have become more like themselves; they chose the life-style characteristics that attract them to others, who exhibit the same behaviors. The chosen characteristics compellingly grow more pronounced and exaggerated, and the chosen clothing, selected by the encircled and threatened personalities, frequently become bizarre. Hairstyles, speech, and other changes harmonize with the chosen group.

Unfortunately, the sought comfort is pathologically limited. The chosen emotional and physical separations are centered on repressed fears that program emotional maladjustments, and they limit, control and shorten lives.

Alarmingly, highly neurotic personalities frequently use a change that is drastic indeed; it voids all other requirements. For example, when obese personalities continually overeat, compelled by strong subconsciously born fears, they eventually gain more weight. And soon, life-threatening, accompanying diseases will develop. Death follows pathologically strong anxieties.

Another physical change personalities, mostly juveniles, program is stooped shoulders. They pathologically somewhat adjust their heights. The adjustments are group-comfort programmed, which are always conscientiously required to allay anxiety and hide inferiority complexes.

Unfortunately, varied personalities' psychological adjustment needs are inexhaustible; the varying demands expand with the personalities' depths and growths. Some are not completely physical, but are obvious changes. Through anxieties, some individuals clumsily alter body movements and co-ordinations. They simply walk, stand, play, or use clumsy body movements, frequently, through preconceived habits or thought patterns formulated by parents or other parental figures. All are subconsciously induced adjustments programmed to reduce anxiety. Within the life-style, personalities view themselves as clumsy and help predict future, body movements. They, with the growing neurosis, have pathologically adjusted to alleviate anxiety. Others, often, emotionally or physically cripple themselves to meet their mental needs. Severely threatened, consciences, centered on personality needs, to distance them selves from anxiety, frequently must alter physical and emotional mobility. The barriers (although life-time enduring) are always timely and coincide with anxiety avoidances, which frequently follow subconsciously induced situational failures fears.

The subconsciously induced emotional growths are never programmed overnight but develop steadily throughout life; the increases are progressively, obsessively demanded by the continually increasing emotional fears and anxieties; they are used universally. Regretfully, a simple use is an extreme over use.

Some personalities alter their bodies positively to disprove strong subconscious fears; some weight lifting, extensive body building exercises are compulsive behaviors, conscientiously demanded by sexually threatened personalities. Many physically over developed males, between forty and fifty years old, die from strokes, heart attacks and other cardiovascular problems.

Those pathological life-style changes are ominously real, for when the repressed fears are viewed realistically, they demand unrealistic, staggering human sufferings. Unfortunately, they frequently accompany harmful psychosomatic diseases. The changes frequently remove individuals from life's mainstream and imprison them in poverty stricken back streets. The lives, built within the compulsively required movements are controlled and perhaps destroyed because individuals become subconscious and conscience captives and live in fear-enclosed seclusions. The barriers, erected for anxiety protection are timely augmented, and they dominate and control lives. The emotionally required physical changes limit lives by programming rigid living guidelines.

In the following chapter, another conscientiously mandated choice, required through fear and anxiety, must be viewed. It, too, is employed to ensure emotional and physical nonparticipation. It's sometime a fear by-product, and it's euphemistically called accidents.

Chapter Five

The Subconscious Mind and Accidents

During the year, Nineteen Hundred and Thirty, a Chicago company drove approximately three million mile annually; its drivers had many accidents, and those accidents increased the company's insurance premium.

The company consequently hired an accident-investigative psychologist, and he discovered that twenty percent of the drivers had eighty percent of the accidents; that correlates with the present streets and highways accidents.

The psychologist recommended that the accident-prone drivers be relieved from their driving requirements and be given interior factory jobs, and later he found that those same individuals had many industrial accidents; eventually he found that those same ones had developed life-threatening diseases, and had ceased having industrial accidents.

The company concluded that the incidences might not be true accidents, and it correctly perceived that some personalities were accident-prone. Then and now the question was and is asked, how and why do personalities become accident-prone?

The answers are found within the subconscious and conscience; frequently when fears are repressed, personalities are formed and personal consuming aggressions follow.

Consequently, the negative, subconsciously repressed material fosters conscious thoughts and feelings that surface during automobile driving. The aggressive conscious thoughts and consequential behaviors are, frequently, conscientiously induced to promote self-punishment. Aggression is a conscientiously induced pathological behavior that is consciously exhibited. Consequently, anger, aggression, and anti-authoritarian attitudes co-exist with many who harbor repressed fears. High-accident-profiled personalities share certain personality traits; impatience is found in all. They disregard good commonsense while driving, and as a neurotic trait, extreme pathologically exhibited impatience is commonly recognized and employed within the driving public. Every state shows it in its vehicular accident reports; it strongly signifies that personalities are neurotic, and the neuroses figure prominently into accidents. It also signifies that personalities are emotionally discontent, and its continual exhibition, within accident-prone situations, is alarmingly compelling. Many drivers are too busy (synonymous with impatience) to drive more slowly and carefully, and thereby, the conscientiously imposed, emotionally immature, impatience-exhibitions program aggressive driving and often produce accidental situations.

It's known that sexual immaturity, found in both male and female drivers, is frequently seen on accident reports. Deep conscientiously induced sexual instabilities program inferiority complexes; highly neurotic, reckless personalities compellingly drive heedlessly to attract public notice, mostly by the opposite sex. All pathologically conscious actions or desires (centered on subconsciously stored, repressed fears and anxieties) are, simply, conscientiously, behaviorally compelled.

Therefore, when personalities persistently seek personal attention, they are exhibiting intensified inferiority complexes programmed by repressed fears. Exaggerated conscious exhibitions such as aggression, anger, impatience, and hostility are neurotic trends and are frequently displayed by drivers; perhaps the term accident-prone, therein originates.

The subconsciously born, conscientiously enforced inferiority complexes have merely programmed different exhibitions, but they, perhaps, are only portraying old self-destructive techniques.

The author found accident-proneness a personal attribute, and prior to therapy, while driving, he found himself frequently, accidentally involved. After therapy, he acquired some recognition of auto-accidental situations.

Perhaps, inferiority complexes' relation to accidents can be broadened because it somewhat explains why some individuals are hurt, while others performing the near identical tasks are not; for instance, why one National Football League running back while carrying the ball is injured, and another carrying the ball, nearly identically, isn't. One is conscientiously accident-prone programmed while the other isn't.

Some personalities deliberately seek others who will physically or emotionally mistreat them; seeking personal mistreatment through relationships is called masochism.

Personalities, ladies mostly, frequently remain with brutal mates, even when it's no longer in their best interest. The author has frequently heard, "I want to go back to him; I deserved the mistreatments." Although, they couldn't explain how the abuse was deserved, they continually returned to poor relationships. Through those and accident-prone situations, personalities deliberately, repetitiously place themselves in accidental and personal-injury situations. Unfortunately, poor judgment is an emotional maladjustment by-product; it and the resultant pseudo-accidents are always stress related, and the conscientiously induced, enforced removals through injury are programmed to ensure nonparticipation. Therefore, through anxiety-related injuries, some personalities are compellingly placed into less stressful and competitive free environments.

Suppose athletes compete while harboring deep conscientiously induced failure fears. Any accident, in that setting, might be termed, anxiety relieving. Maybe it explains why numerous muscle strains, which are compelled through competition fears, occur with many athletes. Therefore, many accidents are circumstantially and individually related because numerous athletes competitively injure body-parts that are circumstantially, competitively, and situationally vital. Carpenters usually injure their primary hand or arm when total incapacitation is required; thumbs or hands are slightly injured when punishment only is pathologically needed. Runners, competing with fears, centered on failure fears, frequently injury leg muscles, laborers hurt backs, and singers suffer voice strains; the incapacitations, simply remove the competitors and thereby alleviate anxieties, somewhat.

The compelling stress-degree could be situational and psychological. The personal stress is always psychologically, pathologically, conscientiously, repressively, and neurotically programmed. Strong emotions cause elevated neurotic exhibitions; they in turn compel anxiety-reduction, stress related behaviorisms. Highly neurotic and psychotic personalities' fears are always unrealistically exaggerated, and living with their deep subconsciously harbored anxieties, they must seek stress-related, avoidance techniques. The erected, intense, subconscious emotional barriers compellingly program stress-reduction removals and situation-displacement avenues; both may promote self-punishment procedures.

When anxieties are elevated, the conscience compellingly programs drastic and dire, escape-orientated behaviorisms. The author once knew a young girl who was raised by elderly parents, who didn't recognize or meet her emotional needs. She abhorred necessitous circumstances. Reaching adulthood, she married an older man, who was somewhat successful; his work necessitated both interstate and intrastate traveling. Subsequently, she became lonely and sought other male companionship, and she soon became convinced her marriage was a mistake. Being unwilling to leave her advantaged life-style, she frequently cried that she could not support herself. She then consciously sought someone who would support her; after several affair failures, she became depressed and sought a psychiatrist who recommended shock treatments; she refused therapy that could help her. Shock treatments programmed to force people to forget repressed fears, strongly prevent subconscious to conscious transfers. Her conscience orchestrated a dreadful, painful, and incomprehensible escape; she, while very young, died from breast cancer.

Deaths, diseases and accidents are not necessarily related but can be consequentially required by ragging anxieties. Many experts feel that accident-prone individuals are also suicidal; drinking and driving is an accident-prone, perfect example. The drinkers may not be seeking death, but driving with elevated speeds program tragic results; alcohol consumption and poorly self-serving neurotic behaviors are terrible partners.

Therefore, individuals should carefully scrutinize thoughts and emotions before acting. Strong emotionally supported thoughts, especially those centering on unsafe driving, combined with drinking, frequently change lives drastically. The conscience, the strong emotional enforcer and conscious thought supplier, frequently sends messages to personalities with inferiority complexes that they are unworthy and sinful. Personalities with strong, intense inferiority complexes frequently harbor thoughts of jumping off high buildings, shooting themselves, or driving into objects at high speeds. Obviously, the thoughts are terribly irresponsible, but yet entirely human.

As our society numerically increases, driving accidents will also increase, and drinking and driving will no doubt dominate many accident-scenes, which are largely calls for help. If help is given, it will frequently come with court dates, fines and useless law enforcement rhetoric.

Home and occupational accidents also rank high in individuals' injury statistics. They are, also, frequently, conscientiously induced through personal discontentment, and individuals are frequently, permanently disabled and must live with their reminders; the non-permanently disabled, often must compellingly seek other anxiety shielding behaviors. Those other methods can be somber indeed, as future chapters will show.

Chapter Six

The Subconscious Mind and Correctional and Mental Institutions

As our society grows, the demands for additional correctional and mental facilities alarmingly increase, and our leaders delightedly ask for more money; our folly continues.

The author interned in the county jail while working toward a Masters Degree, and he found that inmates were mostly mentally ill; society simply incarcerated them, without treating the mental illnesses. The author was accepted by the inmates, but somewhat rejected by the jail guards. The inmates mostly wanted psychotherapy, and they frequently spoke of getting well and avoiding jails.

While passing through the hospital area one day, the author was stopped by an inmate, who sought therapeutic help. After the initial interview, the inmate was told that his file would be sought and a reply given. The file showed that the inmate came from a family of fourteen siblings; each child had a different father. Every father figure showed the same characteristics: they all drank alcohol, and frequently, physically and emotionally mistreated the mother and children.

Consequently, the inmate physically matured with a strong, neurotically formed poor self-esteem, and had frequented many correctional institutes, while consciously exhibiting strong suicidal tendencies: his right and left arms were scarred from the wrist to the elbow with self-inflected knife wounds, and his waist had a solid scar from one side to the other.

His poor self-esteem was startling. After he asked, "Can I be helped," he was told, "Yes, if permission was granted." The inmate merely stated a strong desire to get well; he never mentioned any shortening of jail time.

Shortly after the interview, the author was called to the phone and talked to the inmate's attorney who was informed about the inmate's family history. Immediately after the conversation, the author was called to the county psychiatrist's office. There the author was accused of undermining the criminal judicial system, and was refused permission to treat the inmate. The author was also told if any part of the inmate and author's conversation appeared on the inmate's records, the author would fail. The author was also told that it was the county psychiatrist's job to ensure that inmates were convicted and transferred to the states' correctional institute, emotionally unchanged. The author could only ask, "what am I doing here?"

Until the internship was completed, the student-author could only treat the criminally compelled psychotics who were incapable of emotionally improving, without strong, unavailable medications.

The author found that the entire criminal justice system, including the country psychiatrist, had no criminal rehabilitation plan or desire. The criminal justice system's individuals spent their time doing paper work; while ensuring that the inmates' emotional temperaments were unchanged. That, of course, helped keep recidivism high and criminal justice jobs more secure. The system seemingly exacts revenge, largely ignores convict rehabilitation, and escalates criminal justice costs; therefore convict recidivism increases, which necessitates additional jail and penitentiary needs.

The author also found that the inmates and guards' personalities were alarmingly near identical; deep anger dominated their personalities. The jail atmosphere seemingly attracts angry individuals who use the system to enact revenge, or prove a personal agenda.

Unfortunately, the inmates are frequently beaten; it's euphemistically called discipline. The author once sat next to a younger patron and asked him what he was seeking in life. He answered that he wanted to be a police officer; his job would be to apprehend crooks and punish them on the way to jail to insure that the crooks would not evade justice within a liberal system. Jail guards frequently told the author; that if he would only turn his back, for about two hours, the inmates would never return to jail.

Our society demands full and harsh justice, applicable to others only, but it pleads for mercy when personally applied. Unfortunately, justice administered through revenge only, programs anxiety, anger and rage; released convicts frequently vent those neurotic emotions on an unsuspecting society.

The same system is somewhat employed in the public schools. The students are expected to obey the rules entirely, while the faculty is largely exempt. Student disciplines are largely physical and punitive. Police officers ignore the laws they enforce, and congressmen, personally exempt themselves from many laws they enact.

The same mentality is used within our mental institutions because there, too, the victims are simply fleeing from anxiety, which takes them to institutions where they are misunderstood; unfortunately, the necessary flight began with simple repressions, and soon anxiety and rage appeared. Within the institutions, the patients are mistreated; it's euphemistically called shock therapy, which forces a strong, sudden electric current into patients' brain. Supposedly, it makes patients forget, but the author has seen patients who couldn't remember their names but still showed rage, anxiety and fear.

The author has frequently heard psychiatrists justify shock and other inhumane treatments through meaningless statistics, and they claimed that patients' showed decreases of depression, but they have never proven that patients have less mental gloom, or show improved inferiority complexes.

The author treated a patient who was given ten different shock treatments, against his will. He then reached through the bars and tried to choke his psychiatrist, who promptly ruled the patient needed no more shock. Years later, the patient spent hours recalling subconsciously repressed events; shock treatments made the process infinitely more tedious.

If there are cures for both mental patients and correctional inmates, they must come from consciously resurfacing repressed mental fears. The repressed fears rarely have present reality relevance, but imprison personalities, while programming neurotic and frequently psychotic physical and emotional over-reactions.

The inmates were rarely committed because they were psychotic, but usually for embarrassing someone. Within the institution, they seldom deal with their repressed fears, and thereby don't change the personality patterns that programmed psychotic behavior.

The victims simply become more behaviorally, emotionally rigid and severely limit all selective chances for adjusted behavioral. As the anxieties increase, the consciences must program additional, individual safeguard measures to protect the personalities. The sufferers simply become more psychotic, and further retreat within themselves; completely isolated from all healthy emotional rehabilitation; the patients' consciences have become their worst enemies.

Rehabilitation of both the inmates and the committed patients is a needed goal. The psychotics or highly neurotics can be helped with the aid of modern medicine. Through it, both groups can be medicated to a somewhat normal state. While there, they can be therapeutically treated; they simply transfer subconscious repressions to the conscious. The inmates can also be helped, those that desire, through the same process, without medication. Interestingly, a serial killer was interviewed on why he killed, and he compared his strong, irresistible impulse to a crocodile rising from the bottom to eat and then settling for a while, then rising to eat again. This strong conscientiously enforced need of the killer can be treated by subconscious to conscious fear transfers. Left to fester, beyond youth, the urges intensify, and a killer is formed through his own fears and ideations.

The author has no issue with the death penalty. When it's judged appropriately no rehabilitation is required, but within the present environment it's seldom administered equally to all classes of individuals. Discriminately, American justice, seemingly, is not shared equally by all personalities. There is a great disparity endured between the rich defendants and the poor, as well as the harsh justices administered to the different races. Several prosecuting attorneys have apparently, knowingly used false evidence to aid or enhance doubtful convictions. Obviously, prosecuting attorneys frequently show similar neurotic characteristics with others within the common professional grouping.

But, when individuals are convicted of lesson offences, they will likely be freed. Let the sentences be fully served, and help inmates vocationally and educationally improve themselves: make prison libraries more modern and accessible, and encourage education because most convicts lack high school education. Teach and encourage vocational or professional education to willing inmates. Hire capable therapists and encourage personality reorientation, because when repressed fears are consciously recalled, the inmates' inferiority complexes will automatically diminish. Finally, separate those who don't want personal improvements from those who do. When treated, inmate's anger levels are reduced; separating the prisoners will be easy. Reducing anger levels; lowering inferiority complexes; and changing neurotic behaviors can't be accomplished through confinements, corporal punishments, or shock treatments. There must be other ways.

Chapter Seven

The Subconscious Mind and Substance Dependences

Drug usages (including alcohol, the most biologically destructive drug) predominately figure in most incarcerations, addictions and drug dependences; all are a consequence of continual drug use. Many students, teachers, doctors, and experts, believe that addictions or dependences are simply biological, yet, most reliable evidence and credible testimony support the beliefs of psychological dependencies; they, in turn, help promote biologically formed physical habits. The author has cured many drug dependencies with therapeutic interventions, and all drug related problems and habits disappear immediately following relevant subconscious to conscious transfers.

The dependents' symptomatic behaviors while withdrawing from drugs will shed additional light on the debate. There, one gets a clear view that most habitual users strive for years to kick the dependencies, and accompanying habits; they are told that they are hopelessly intolerant and dependant for life. Perhaps with most treatments, it's true, but there is another way, which frightens many but cures addictions and dependencies. Read on.

Before curing, addicts or dependants must understand the word addiction, which simply means to be enslaved to a habit, to be inclined or dependent on a substance. Scrutinized, the wording implies a psychological dependency, which consequently programs biological behaviors.

Obviously, personalities become dependent on substances through continual usages; the intolerances are programmed through subconsciously born, conscientiously induced emotional desires and the creation of the drugs' physical tolerance; the users take drugs to attain emotional needs to reduce anxiety. Then, personalities take drugs from physical and emotional needs, both are conscientiously controlled. Consequently, satisfying those needs, the drugs' quantity must compellingly be increased; the pathologically driven strong desires and substance usages program the dependences.

There are, of course, many substances that through use, easily form dependencies; their licit or illicit status bears no relationship to their strengths, biologically harmful factors, or their availabilities. Money, politics, availabilities, and human emotions control the drug demands, while one drug, alcohol, is strongly prominent in its demand and availability; it also is number one in harming the human body. Its producers minimize its habit-forming, dependant-qualities.

Factually, alcohol consumption programs more social damage than all the other drugs combined; it figures prominently in the majority of inmate confinements: fifty percent of all murders were committed when the murderers or victims were intoxicated. Most passionate crimes were committed when the perpetrators or victims were inebriated. Estimations assert that there are ten to twenty million alcoholics nationally, but when the weekend and other problem drinkers are included, the figure could rise to forty million or more; those personalities, too, are hastening to be totally dominated by drug use.

Since personalities permit substances to dominate their lives, the question arises, why? Since the drugs shorten, restrict, and dominate their existences, why do they use them? The answers are found by examining both the users and their dependencies.

Foremost, all intolerances are identical, and the symptoms' degrees of withdrawal vary only with the individuals' pathological need for substance, which is always centered on personal neurotic growths.

The dependants' emotions trigger the strength of intensities and the length of time of intolerance; then, they are dependent because they are users and are neurotic. Substance strengths, alone, don't cause dependencies; experts contend that well-adjusted individuals become drug intolerant less. Maybe they use or abuse harmful substances less frequently.

Unfortunately the subconscious (the repressed fear storehouse) programs all dependencies, and the conscience directs the functions; neurotic personalities, subconsciously programmed, thereby control the dependant degrees and required time of usage.

Personalities become obsessed with substances, sex, food and liquids; many have stated, "I don't have a problem; I simply like to use alcohol, have sex, eat food, or use drugs." Then, intolerances are psychological and not biological. The immature neurotics employ a substance, use sex, or excessively eat food to satisfy emotional, pathologically elevated needs and desires, intensified by anxieties. The users employ and increase the pathologically needed substances until dependences are programmed; their usages become the emotional crutches.

Dependents frequently say, "I need a drink. I'm going out and get drunk." Their usages briefly consummate emotional containments and contentment's. A wealthy friend of the author said, "I drink scotch because it's a manly drink." The flip side to his obsession is, he doesn't feel manly without scotch. Without the usages, the neurotics feel emotionally and sexually inadequate. The discontentments are conscious-feelings programmed by subconsciously harbored anxieties; the conscience always strives to pathologically shield the personality. Simply, personalities respond to consciously felt inadequacy feelings. Repressed fears and anxiety, formed by juveniles, are almost totally adult irrelevant, but are brought forward throughout life; juvenile fears become adult anxieties, and substance usages are centered on those anxieties, which are programmed by consciously felt pathological desires and continual substance increases. The consequential processes are called dependencies.

Within the young, emotional needs begin. Juvenile inferiority complexes erect strong barriers against increasing anxieties; the pathologically strengthening complexes demand more stringent, conscientiously enforced desires. Subconsciously born fears and anxieties consequently program strong consciously felt demands; personalities use substances and form behaviorisms to counter the growing anxieties, and the efforts are somewhat successful. Unfortunately, the desired relaxation is temporary; the crutches' strengths then must be increased because the neurotically, compulsively, emotionally, and intensified wants and needs must be satisfied.

If the dependant's emotional issues are left un-addressed, strong demands remain. Therefore, when desired substances are deprived, abusers are compelled to use other drugs. Since all substances' uses are subconsciously born and conscientiously enforced, additional-psychological-needs and desires are then programmed.

Dependant's physical withdrawal symptoms are mostly, commonly, consciously shared: they frequently perspire profusely, and heart palpitations and physical weaknesses quickly follow; involuntary kicking and regurgitating are also witnessed. With eyes watering profusely, their noses pass mucous, accompanied by stuttering, illogical speech, shortening of breath, and violent shaking. They often develop delirium tremors, and goose flesh appears. Their eyes dilate, and food appetites disappear. They become irritable, yawn violently, and also develop diarrhea and abdominal cramps. Since every behavior is conscientiously directed, they immediately disappear when the pathologically subconscious reasons are removed.

Unfortunately, until addressed and removed, the behavioral problems remain and increase, but the users and society want simplified cures; many poorly thought-out programs now exist. Within each, the dependants are hospitalized and withdrawn form the abused substance. During the detoxification-period, users are then bombarded with substance-propaganda, and many such facilities give mild shock treatments to hurry the process. The average stay is about six weeks; while there, users are brainwashed about the programs' merits.

They are then told that they are cured and can re-enter society, but the pathologically repressed fears and consequently programmed anxieties have been ignored through greed, indifference, and lack of knowledge. Unfortunately the dependants have to re-enter society burdened with the same ragging inferiority complexes that necessitated the habitual substance usages and intolerances; expectedly, recidivism will be near one hundred percent.

Sadly, dependants, seeking help, never consciously transfer repressed subconscious fears; with anxieties left untreated, they soon return to the substances abuses. They are then told repetitiously that they are abnormally incurable.

Alcohol and nicotine dependencies have been successfully treated many times. Following therapy, both groups were able to lead drug-free lives. Unfortunately, alcoholics, and other drug users, frequently preferred the drug culture rather than face a therapeutic uncertainly. Frequently, alcoholics' emotional problems are centered on sexual insecurities, just as the friend and his compulsion for scotch.

A lifetime friend was a smoker and an alcoholic. Although he frequently addressed his smoking habit, he never sought help for his alcoholism. After years of excessive drinking and smoking, along with an accompanying personal economic decline, the friend died of a brain tumor. Another alcoholic friend frequently consumed a case of beer daily, and while intoxicated he tried to kill his young son; after therapy, he became a model father and husband.

Unfortunately, alcohol has become stereotyped in most societies. Many personalities believe that alcohol and fun are inseparable. Alcohol advertisings suggest that individuals are sexier when drinking, which makes it dangerous because juveniles are more easily convinced.

The same thinking is seen in the drug culture, for the users, too, are highly neurotic personalities who strive for group togetherness; they adopt the same clothing and hairstyles while seeking group comfort.

Since emotional problems and intolerances are commonly shared, the adopted life-styles are compellingly compulsive, and any consequential anxiety reduction is only temporary; the strong-drug demands will always excite other substance needs.

The reasons for individuals' drug-usages and the consequential usages expose our governments' failing drug-enforcement policy. Some things are obviously true; the drug war can't be won when it's waged through education, only. It must be waged against all drug usages, and it also will not be won when fought from legal or moral points only, or when erroneous or totally false information is primarily used.

Early in the twentieth century alcohol-use was unconstitutional; the law was unenforceable because of the pathological reasons for increased usages programmed by and through the neurotically strong needs for drugs. When deprived of selected drugs, neurotics simply use others; the government seemingly doesn't have a clue to its cause or cure. Thereby if the war is won, it must address and educate personalities, and subconscious to conscious fear transfers are essential.

Clearly, drug use is personal, and several individuals figure in the drug-use equation: relatives, friends, doctors, and perhaps some selected others; governments should have no say unless requested. The governments' belief that it knows best is entirely ridiculous.

Truthfully, all substance usages are pathologically employed to alleviate anxiety, and many habitual behaviors are used for identical purposes. Unfortunately, the strongest pathologically enforced needs are food and sex, and the intense desires are centered on neurotic emotions; excessive food use becomes biologically destructive. Its dependent qualities are recognizably difficult; the basic food desires are conscientiously directed with some minor conscious alterations. Educational journals ridiculously teach that nutritional appetites are autonomously controlled. Unfortunately, without subconsciously repressed fear alterations, the nutritional personality demands augment.

Nutritionally enlarged needs are more dangerous as they are incorporated in a vital requirement. Unfortunately, the compelling desires frequently demand an enlarged quantity of the more fatty foods. The compulsions are destructive, and when dietary systems attack conscious nutritional demands, only, they always fail. They ignore the repressed fears that are stored within the subconscious, and the brain-part that stores the anxieties, which also controls sexual desires, nutritional demands, and thirst needs; abuses frequently follow. All three pathological needs are, somewhat, socially encouraged: the obese are bombarded daily with food messages; endless alcoholic advertisings stimulate alcoholics; and half-nude male and female bodies, frequently shown on television, remind over-sexed personalities of their problems. Dependency failures are expected because the abuses are programmed within the subconscious, experienced consciously, and accepted normally; individuals merely grow like themselves. Naturally all intolerances, including nutritional, sexual and thirst, start and augment through repetitious repressions. Consequently, inferiority complexes compel personalities to live with the substances' attractions. Unfortunately, strong fears (programmed by repressions) create strong anxieties, and compellingly needs and desires program and expand the intolerances. Thereby, variant subconsciously formed emotions compliantly vary needs with different personalities. The ragging anxieties, through conscientious direction, promote strong desires, and augment the maladaptive needs, which become lifetime crutches.

Unfortunately, elevated wants and desires are universal, and they will only grow and intensify. The accompanying life-styles, and the programmed physical changes that limit and control lives and program additional bizarre habits, indicate that personalities are reacting to extreme anxiety.

Living within bodies, while exhibiting imperfect personalities, individuals are dominated by ragging anxieties, which promote gross dependencies on alcohol and other drugs, and they also show hair loss, dress near identically, and gregariously frequent commonplaces. The men frequently wear facial hair and earrings; while women wear short dresses, change hair color, and use other attention drawing behaviors. All adopted life-style behaviors simply indicate that the personalities are neurotic. Obviously, the life-style inhabitants are seeking help without the knowledge. All help, if it comes, must be timely, because injuries and sicknesses always follow strong emotions.

In time, untreated strong emotions intensify, and they always demand more severe future dire consequences. Emotional intensifications always increase drug usage and augment the withdrawal problems. In time the abusers will compellingly adopt other physical, anxiety-shielding methods, which, factually, strives to lesson the dread-shrouded, pathologically induced performances. As previously stated, the conscience computes the emotional and physical shields between repressed fears and the personality. Thereby noncompliances are somewhat personally soothing, but unfortunately the personalities also become more rigid, complacent, and emotionally distraught. They have become more like themselves.

Normally, every one is psychologically substance dependent or behaviorally (habits) physically addicted, which poorly serves positive adult behavior. The consequential, pathological disorders always predated adulthood, and the timely, juvenile-orientated fears and anxieties always indicate the presence of neurosis. The strong emotions and accompanying physical handicaps, which are timely grouped, portray strong individualistic and socialistic indictments. The social indictments are against the government that has allowed its citizens to reach adulthood with no human psychological knowledge.

The penalties are many and varied because money is spent on useless experiments, poorly thought out counseling methods, and psychological misadventures. All coordinate the consequential human suffering, and unfortunately, lives are frequently left unfulfilled and shortened.

Accordingly, public psychological education is absolutely required. Many citizens are grossly overweight and oversexed, while showing many other emotional discontent symptoms. Consequently, they hasten to premature and painful deaths.

Chapter Eight

The Subconscious Mind and Vocations and Professions

Individuals' vocational and professional selections have always perplexed most societies; although they will severely affect lives, the decisions are still mostly left to chance. What is even more insidious, they're frequently selected emotionally. The process, although cognitively viewed, is dominated emotionally within the subconscious. Consequently, personalities are frequently locked into vocations and professions that limit their futures, and unfortunately that often remains factual for a lifetime. Obviously, not all vocational and professional choices are poorly made, but many are pathological byproducts.

Interestingly, many personalities are more limited by their strong emotions than by their abilities. The author researched an article written by several doctors, who divided a study group into three smaller groups: the original grouping was drawn from three sources: a leading university, a mental institution, and a vocational training school. The three separate groups were tested first on intelligence and were found to be about equal.

They were then given a psychological profile test; the results startled the doctors: first, there were no discernable differences between vocational school students' and the mental institutional inmates' psychological profile scores. Second, there were vast differences found between the college students' test scores and the other two groups. Accordingly, the doctors wrote that if students felt that they could make it, they usually went to college.

Public school and college dropouts are fairly common with young people, and failure fears, financial, and many other problems figure in the equation. Unfortunately, many students frequently select the easier choice, and almost unbelievably, high school officials frequently misdirect minority students' vocational and professional selections; evidence shows that frequently minority students are misguided from colleges and professions into vocations.

Interestingly, individuals within professions bear similar and startling personality characteristics: certain personality types are attracted to certain fields; for instance, lawyers portray similar personality patterns. The leading universities seemingly encourage aggression in their applicants; lawyers feel no remorse about lying and distorting; they show much greed. Several attorneys, after successful psychological therapy, left the profession knowing that typical, pathological, neurotic attorney behavior was no longer personally acceptable.

Accordingly, only highly neurotic individuals become bill collectors; they often portray extreme cynicism.

Police departments frequently attract applicants who bear grudges against society and choose that field to vent their anger. Many have an authoritarian complex; wearing a gun turns them on, and they give orders easily, but take them poorly. They all too frequently mistreat prisoners, and there is very little, or no, emotional-personality differences between the jail inmates and the guards; they, indeed, show that they have repressed approximately the same fears and have developed the same pathological needs. Tremendous stress is shown within both groups, and enlarged inferiority complexes are portrayed; physical and emotional suffering are demandingly endured. Obviously, emotionally immature personalities, exhibiting extreme inferiority complexes, fill the jails. Only their dress, differentiate the two groups.

The athletic field frequently attracts athletes who have personal-sexuality doubts, and they, to prove their sexuality, are frequently attracted to the more violent-sports. Physically disproving patho-logical-inferiority feelings (born within the subconscious), they strive to distant themselves from anxieties. Accordingly, both male and female homosexuals, pursuing sexual identities, are frequently found in the more violent and physical sports. There certainly are more women competing in physically, demanding sports.

Male and female personalities (harboring deep, enlarged inferi-ority feelings) encompass the prostitution field; they frequently feel that they deserve emotional and physical punishment, and must remain within the field. Within it, they strive to prove they won't carry out some strongly repressed fears. Unfortunately, they fre-quently attract the opposite sex, and they, too, are striving to dis-prove the same fears; the personalities, programmed to allay anxie-ties, are almost identical. Unfortunately, the chosen field will only increase anxieties; violence is predicable.

The boxing sport attracts similar personality profiles, and its inhabitants portray intense frustration and anger; behavioral studies suggest that many doubt their personal sexuality and spend time inflaming their opponents by calling them fags. Most frequently, when people repetitiously question others' sexuality, the question-ers harbor deeply repressed sexuality fears. The sport is crowded with extremely maladjusted individuals; the strong emotional dis-content is evident.

The medical profession, frequently, attracts similar personality types: abnormal greed and physical-medical supremacy beliefs are foremost. Some can be bought; other fields frequently call them prostitutes. They seemingly are biological-medical-profession brainwashed, and have exaggerated self-importance attitudes. Some feel that they are infallible, and they all exhibit a brain-

washed demeanor of treating the physical body and essentially ignoring the subconscious and conscience directions of all diseases.
Unfortunately, they exhibit many emotional problems, and their
adopted life-styles are pathologically induced; they and all human-
ity share common and strong neurotic symptoms; many are addicted to drugs. Medical doctors live average-time spans; they
blame medical stress, even though stress is consciously exhibited,
but is-always and only-subconsciously formed. Neurotic medical
personalities merely portray the personally felt insecurities.

The German Nazi political movement, portraying extreme aggression, attracted many highly neurotic and psychotic individuals,
who were mostly social outcasts. Vast unlimited-violence seemingly attracted them; personal immunity, played its part. Within the
violent movement, they lived out their fantasies, proving their repressed fears where inconsequential. Their animosity (vented toward others, a common trait) programmed history.

The religious movement seemingly attracts those who share
much personal guilt. They are, hopefully, trying to prove that relig-
ion might expunge their deep psychological problems. There is no
right or wrong implied; and much good is accomplished within
various religious movements. But, great personalities choose the
field and thereby strive to disprove the deeply felt pathological
fears. The subconsciously born, deep primary fears, and the personalities involved, program the scenario.

Students and scholars who enter counseling and therapy professions, basically, have near identical goals: they seemingly share
much personal guilt. Along with dentists, they have large suicidal
incidences, and the vocation is filled with those who seek self-
forgiveness through public service. Somehow, they expect their
personal, pathological, psychological problems will disappear, but
unfortunately, personal intervention therapy is almost never considered; they too share extreme guilt complexes, and the diminished
self-evaluations orchestrate the high suicide rates.

The list is endless; unfortunately, many personalities don't choose a profession or vocation with clear, decisive reasoning, but do so through strong subconsciously born emotions.

Those decisions, along with strong emotions, frequently start very early; many young personalities show emotional problems and selectively remove themselves from school and society, although schools largely control societies. The important decisions will greatly control lives; future employment, and chosen neighborhoods will be limited.

Compellingly, personalities choose mates, homes, schools, and vocations with strong emotions: the sexually insecure males select the best-built females for mates, and many immature ones select the more physically demanding vocations. Mostly, they are simply proving that they will not perform the dreaded fear; frequently, striving to prove the repressions never happened, and the anxieties don't exist.

Some procedures must be changed. Is any society really humane? The changes must come within the subconscious. Vocational and professional choices, largely pathologically made, should be more severely scrutinized; poor choices increase frustration and augment internal intensifications.

Chapter Nine

The Subconscious Mind and the Bodies' Immune Systems

Modern medicine has drawn a somewhat up beat decision, as doctors and patients now practice conscious-living wills. Unfortunately, the conscious resolve is never sufficient because it must accompany subconscious health. The conscience directs the body's immune system, and it consequently dictates physical health; it, thereby, manages the acquiring, maintaining, and the ultimate biological prevention of all diseases. Although the immune system is the weapon against every disease, the conscience makes all decisions, including life or death; strong emotions (programmed by repressions and consequently formed anxieties) force many of its directions.

Medical doctors are very learned about the body and its diseases, but they apparently know nothing about conscience orchestrations, as they, seemingly, never look beyond the biological body. Through indifference, lack of knowledge and greed, they completely ignore most mind concepts except independent-body malfunctions and diseases. Factually, life is a miracle; personalities live within bodies and control them somewhat consciously, while ignoring the conscience. Even the conscious body controls have conscience-border-line dominations.

The conscience not only directs the body's immune systems, but the subconscious (the consciences' home) also houses all repressed fears and anxieties. The conscience programs the inner workings; essentially, subconsciously formed, strong emotions disrupt immune systems' functions. The body's many immune-system components work toward homeostasis (maintaining healthy balance), but strong anxieties frequently disrupt and change the healthy balance.

The outer skin layers form the primary germ barrier. The immune systems begin with the lymphatic vessels, many small lymphatic tissue masses, which are the following: lymphatic tissue, lymphatic nodes, and three organs (tonsils, thalamus, and the spleen). Primarily, the lymphatic systems capture lymph that escapes the capillaries, but they also transfer digestive fat to the blood, produce lymphocytes, and develop antibodies. Additionally, the systems have small vein like structures, found throughout bodies, which functionally fight infection. The entire system obtains and retains homeostasis.

The skin (the dermis and epidermis) presents formidable outer bacterial barriers. The epidermis, composed of closely packed cells, contains keratin, and when bodies perspire, the perspiration washes bacteria away.

A mucus membrane, within bodies, lines each organ; it keeps the bodies' cavities moist, and captures many microbes, which enter the digestive tract.

The nose has mucus-lined hairs that filter air and trap microbes; the eyes timely blink and produce protectoral tears. When microbes invade the eyes, tears wash them away and prevent colonization. Salvia washes teeth and prevents microbes from uniting, which are then flushed and destroyed in the digestive tract.

A small cartilage, the epiglottis, shields the voice box while swallowing, and prevents the microbes from entering the respiratory tract. The urine flow protects against microbes entering the urinary tract, where gastric liquid (hydrochloric acid, some enzymes, and much mucus) destroy others.

If viruses invade bodies, cells are attacked; the injured cells produce a protein called, interferon, which causes other uninjured cells to fight all viruses.

Complement, an eleven proteins group found in almost all blood serum, fights infections, aids many immune and allergic functions, and promotes antibody productions. Properdin, another protein-compound found in serum, combined with compliment, destroys certain bacteria.

When invading microbes evade other defensive lines, they encounter phagocytosis (a cell group, which ingests and destroys them).

When microbes damage body tissue, inflammation develops; it's called fever.

The increased body temperature promotes some body functions that aid repairs; it represents an additional barrier. Commonly, they are all aimed at immunity.

Antigens, chemical substances that cause antibody formations, unite with the antibodies and program changes. Having two characteristics, they program antibodies' formations and consequently unite with them; comprised with both abilities, they are complete, and they, combined with an antigen, form a potent weapon against bacterium or bacterial groups.

Lymphocytes (two related, sensitized-cell compounds) protect bodies against bacteria, fungus, toxins, and other invading-objects. The cells attach and destroy invading bacterium; the process is called, cellular immunity. Additionally, bodies producing circulating antibodies that kill other viruses and bacteria are called, humoral immunities.

Miraculously, all disease-and infection-immunities program and maintain homeostasis. Medical professionals perhaps are taught that bodies are primary; Christians are taught differently. Minds are supreme; bodies are subservient. With all the bodies' disease barriers, they will only stay disease or infection free while the subconscious minds are healthy.

Bodies' complete compounds for disease and infection defenses are perfect, but remain subservient to strongly repressed subconscious fears and emotions; thereby, older individuals become sick more frequently than younger ones. As personalities age, subconsciously repressed fears (augmented through time and additional repressions) increasingly interfere with normal, healthy body functions; normal homeostasis is disrupted, and the living will has been altered.

Perhaps this explains why elderly married couples suffer, closely, time-related deaths. The will to live remains intact while both live, but when either one dies, anxiety increases within the subconscious of the living one, and death soon follows.

From immune systems to diseases, poor or good health is always found. The following chapter should answer some questions.

Chapter Ten

The Subconscious Mind and Disease

If minds, combined with strong emotions (fear, rage and anxiety) alter normal, healthy body functions, they also program many diseases. Obviously, then, personalities direct their own futures through repressions, which consequently cause strong emotions; their individualities are expensive, but unfortunately, reconstruction therapy is frightening.

The author developed and kept ulcers throughout his undergraduate studies. He also suffered from allergies, asthma, and had rheumatoid arthritis in both hands. At thirty, his stomach was surgically repaired; he was consumed with rage.

Dr. Milton Alvis, a medical doctor and heart specialist was recommended; he used hypnotherapy, and the author entered the program with much trepidation.

Several years' later, allergic reactions, asthmatic attacks, rheumatoid arthritis, and stomach disorders were completely removed; the experience was both emotional, and miraculous.

The word disease is derived from two words: first, *dis-*, meaning not; second, *-ease* means to be relaxed. The entire word means uneasy. Obviously, our forefathers knew the true meaning, and the word implies that the diseases are programmed through emotional discomfort.

Disease lists are vast; just as human personalities are varied. Perhaps, the more recognized psychosomatic diseases should be written about first.

10.1 ALLERGIES, ASTHMA, HAY FEVER AND HIVES

By 1953, most leading universities psychosomatically grouped the diseases, allergies, asthma, hay fever, and hives, with the word, psychosomatic, which literally means that the mind and body are equal, yet they are not because the mind is the master, and the body is subservient.

The body simply responds to conscious and conscientious innovations. The broader meanings of psychosomatics refer to the psyche and its influence on diseases. The diseases' severity or their reoccurrences don't change their psychosomatic relationships. While enduring the more frequently known neurotically formed diseases: gastric ulcers, cardiovascular disorders, and allergies; suffers learn that they are mentally and physically painful, limiting, and frequently deadly. Then, the diseases severities will not reveal their physical or mental originations to those living within the bodies; the clues are found within the minds. If patients lose the diseases' symptoms following therapy, then the diseases must be psychosomatic. If well-adjusted personalities endure fewer diseases than the maladjusted, then most diseases must be mentally induced. If life is longer and more delightful without strong emotions, then perhaps all diseases are emotionally, conscientiously induced.

An antigen is any substance that upon being introduced into bodies causes antibiotic productions, or reacts with them; when personalities are antigen over-reactive, they are hypersensitive or allergic, and allergens program the over-reaction process. Any substance, combined with neurosis, can become an allergen, and the more common are coffee, tea, chocolate, penicillin, dust and moles. The diseases shouldn't be taken casually because they frequently destroy lives. Asthma, emphysema, and heart failure killed the authors' younger sister. Anaphylaxis is a common allergic reaction; it literally means protection because it develops in the humoral immune system; an acute reaction can be fatal.

Some other allergic reactions are the following: hay fever, bronchial asthma, hives, and dermatitis.

They are all allergic reactions, and they represent over-reactions to allergens; they additionally represent bodies consciously exhibiting conscience directions promoted by anxieties. Simply, the conscience promotes allergic reactions to alleviate anxieties.

Bronchial asthma, by its nature, is the more dangerous, for with it, the patient has trouble exhaling; spasms of the bronchi and some smooth muscles program the problem. With the increased exhaling problems, alveoli (small hollow lung openings) inflate and remain enlarged. The mucus membranes (that line the airways) become irritated and secrete excessive mucus, which prevents normal bronchi and bronchiole functions.

As suffers breath less oxygen, blood becomes deprived of oxygen, and the heart must beat faster. Obviously a prolonged asthmatic attack can promote extreme heart trouble.

10.2 EMPHYSEMA

Asthma also seemingly aids developments of emphysema; the consequential air and gas storages promote lung swelling, and with the expansion, they lose the ability to absorb oxygen, Alveoli, lung air sacs, become damaged; air and gas accelerations and accumulations quickly follow.

Oxygen diffusion is hindered across alveolar-capillary membranes as emphysema progresses; alveoli are replaced with diseased connective tissue, and oxygenated blood is reduced. Patients suffer shortness of breath, and carbon dioxide accumulates.

Emphysema and asthma are frictional and seemingly are causa-
tively connected. The medical profession views cigarette usages,
and all air pollutions as originally significant.

Mostly, asthma attacks are allergic reactions, and the word
anaphylaxis means against one's self. The immune system main-
tains homeostasis, but with asthma and allergies, the bodies' defense works against homeostasis. Neurotic personalities, with allergies, are fighting themselves; simply, the anger and rage they show,
or hide, are subconsciously born because their repressed fears program consciously felt anxieties. Personalities handle the consequential anger in several ways: some wear their feelings outwardly
and explode easily, while others suppress them, hide the causes and
die inwardly. Both extremes are deadly; because one dies inwardly
and the other dies confrontationally.

Repetitious repressions promote inner tensions, which are exhibited through psychosomatic reactions. Personalities have selected,
through conscience programming, the proper medical and allergic
responses. Allergies, then, are merely neuroses' advanced exhibition forms, and when neuroses are left untreated, tensions increase;
allergies will augment. When medically treated, by immunization,
only, the psychological causes are ignored; tense consciences must
select other allergens to alleviate ragging anxieties.

Interestingly, allergy suffers are labeled as weeping inside, as
their symbolic crying (watery eyes and running noses) emulate
emotional conscious misery.

Personalities live within bodies and consciously control them
somewhat, and the limited physical movements are viewed as natural. The consciences' direct requirements are more believably difficult and are largely ignored and misnamed.

A brilliant graduate student once told the author, "They just
happen." She endured an allergic reaction to cedar-pollen yearly
and called it a happenstance. Bodies (in pollen responses) through
conscience controls create antibodies, which consequently program

certain biological changes. The student and the medical profession ignore the subconsciously programmed emotions, the conscience directions, the tensions that augment, and the seriousness of increased inferiority complex growths. Conscious and conscience biological controls have evolved for centuries, and the miraculous, apparent, universal planning demands a detailed, careful order. The perfectly coordinated body structures scientifically incorporate both conscious and conscience controls; both are interwoven with subconsciously formed and programmed thoughts, feelings, and emotions. Conscientiously induced positive thoughts greatly influence biological movements, and negative thoughts and emotions strongly interrupt, limit, and change them. Aging augments emotions, which then alters the conscious and mandates further conscience controls; fear repressions consequently program anxieties, which program rigid personalities.

Neurotically strong, repressed fears program conscientiously erected, strong emotional and physical barriers, which cause inner body intensifications; the neurotically strong inner tensions program sicknesses, accidents and deaths.

The inner tensions are read through blood pressures and other vital body signals, which frequently help produce misinterpretations of organic originations. The subconscious and conscience predate birth, but are largely doubted and ignored; the vital and complex functions are misunderstood and mislabeled. Unfortunately, individuals demand subconscious and conscience perfection and strive to and shamefully hide all pathologically formed imperfections, which always equal the degree and sum of repressions. The subconscious imperfections program sicknesses, perhaps even cancers.

10.3 CANCER

Cancer isn't a simple disease, but a varied complexity. Simplistically, cancer is the continual splitting of a single body cell, and the consequential growth; many and varied body cells produce multiple cancer types.

As the cell division continues to grow, tumors are formed, which are divided into two classes: benign and cancerous (malignant). Malignancy means that the tumor can both grow and spread, and the latter ability is called, metastasis. When the mass can't spread, it's usually, easily removed; with malignant growths, its extraction is much more difficult, and sometimes impossible.

As malignancies grow, they frequently affect other surrounding areas through the following methods: inner mechanical, biological-diseased body-parts pressure, affected and conscience directed malignant cell motility, and the conscientiously controlled malignant cells' toxicity.

Left untreated, the malignant cells will frequently invade the lymph nodes through the blood vessels; accordingly, the gravest and ominous metastatic abilities and problems then arise. The malignant cells, arriving at a different invaded site, frequently an organ, grow uncontrollably and program their own blood and nutrient needs; the organ is consequently crowded and shrinks (atrophies); it will frequently die. In some cases the growth is not only untreatable but, also, locationally difficult.

Cancer is not a new disease. The universally shared fear is partly caused through subject ignorance. The cancer cell types and locations largely govern their names. Thereby, epithelial cells growths are called, carcinomas; connective tissue tumors are called, sarcomas; and skin mole cancer masses are called melanomas.

Leukemia is frequently called blood cancer; with it, victims produce uncontrolled mature and immature white blood cells, which interfere with normal body functions. Patients frequently hemorrhage within vital brain locations, and the mature white blood cell deficiencies program many infections within other body parts; anemia is the results, which reduces the red blood cells' and platelets' normal production.

All cancer causes are largely unknown; the medical profession is struggling with the problem, while devising various treatments. Unfortunately, through lack of knowledge, indifference or greed, it ignores the subconscious and conscience, and their inner functions.

A lady once asked, "When will the medical profession invent a pill to prolong life." The question, of course, was the usual demand for miracle drugs. Unfortunately, no doctor can ever make personalities live, who are literally killing themselves with strong emotions that program drug use and overuse; the true killers and their causes are never considered. By removing themselves from their personal responsibilities and by remaining ignorant about the subconscious and repressed fears, the general public will continually suffer preventable diseases and die premature deaths.

Cancer causes have been linked to air, food, and water; all three are essential. More popular beliefs link cancer to harmful tobacco and alcohol use, frequently, sufficient quantities of either are deadly, but if their usages cause cancer growths, why don't all habitual abusers develop malignancies?

The medical profession teaches that individual cell growths are controlled chemically; the author believes that cell divisions and growths are directed by the pituitary gland, a small gland found at the base of the skull. However, both chemicals and the pituitary are controlled conscientiously, from within the subconscious, and strong emotions, repressed fears, and anxieties are also found there. Some doctors have now found that some patients show strong irrational, pathological anger when they have malignant growths. Simply, stores anxieties interfere with normal mind and body functions.

Patients frequently reveal what they have repressed without knowing it; paranoids, have frequently told that they are afraid they would kill someone, and many terminal patients informed the author that they deserve to die, while others consciously, fought death.

Many others openly showed guilt symptoms from repressed fears, and felt they deserved a horrible death. Malignant tumors, predated by the following: anger (the strong subconsciously born emotion), consequential guilt feelings, anxiety (an intensified emotion), and strong (conscientiously programmed and mandated) inferiority complexes, are additional methods of protecting the personality.

Individuals are living longer and thereby their personalities are growing more intense through repetitious repressions; the subconsciously born cancerous reasons have simply augmented. The conscience programs the growths; if a cure is found, it must enclose the subconscious formed fears, conscience directions, and conscious medicine.

Factually, cancer strikes frequently within entire families, almost as if they are predestined; many doctors believe that individuals inherit cancer pre-dispositions through gene developments, but genes too are directed conscientiously. If cancers are inherited through paternity, fathers lose genetic-direct-biological contact immediately after conception. To assume that one sperm cell programs all paternal-genetic material and thereby orchestrates future, distant malignant growths through genetic control is an extreme unsupportable stretch. Personalities (subconsciously formed and limited through family interchanges), combined with intense anxieties, and the overall conscience moral and ethical growths, more believably, direct the individual disease selection through the bodies' genes. Within that concept, maybe we can retain or regain some sanity.

The Skin and Its Derivates

There are many skin and its derivative diseases; only two will be discussed.

10.4 SYSTEMIC LUPUS

This disease is frequently called lupus because it likely derived its name from the butterfly-like rash that often forms across patients' noses and extends into the cheek area; the rash resembles a wolf's bite.

Occurring mostly in women of childhood-bearing age, the disease can be both dangerous and deadly. It's an autoimmune systematic disease, in which, the immune system is programmed to act against its body parts. Consequently, it damages various-blood-vessels and other body tissues in the lungs, kidneys, liver, and heart.

Lupus frequently strikes in families, and the patients often develop rheumatoid arthritis and rheumatic fever; the medical profession thinks it is genetically induced. The disease is frequently accompanied by paranoia and schizophrenia; high blood pressure is often found.

Obviously, lupus is no simple disease; it frequently strikes within entire families, but isn't contagious. Where found, it often accompanies both rheumatoid arthritis and rheumatic fever, and it's frequently accompanied by neurotic and psychotic emotional disorders. Its inherited aspects have never been proven; genes, of course, have a bearing on biologically transferred diseases, but genes are controlled within the subconscious, and the conscience programs all genetic responses. Only the mind can direct the disease to program the immune system to fight the body; only the mind can direct the disease to attack the kidney, heart, brain, and other body organs; thereby the disease must be subconsciously born, conscientiously directed, and required through personality selections.

Where psychotic behaviors are found, body functions are frequently dysfunctional. With lupus, the immune system fights, rather than, protects the body; homeostasis is destroyed, and all observable evidence indicates that it's psychosomatically induced.

Consequently, lupus patients probably harbor much anger, and they are merely fighting themselves; the bodies involved simply perform the orchestrated tasks.

Children raised in near identical environments with common parents have almost identical personalities; their programmed individualities and biological characteristics will often be almost identical. For instance, two hyper-tensive parents produce hyper-tensive children. It means the personalities are almost identical and common diseases are consequential.

10.5 PSORIASIS

Psoriasis is a disease, which can become very serious; it affects all ages, but mostly adults. It's a skin disease, which can cover the entire body, but usually is found on the elbows, knees and waistbands. Doctors have recently discovered changes in the mitoses rate in epidermal cells, and anxiety and psoriasis are frequently paired; unfortunately, tension indicates self-imposed guilt, and, consequently, consciences must act to alleviate the inner stress. The cell changes, too, are related to the turmoil.

Doctors suspect that it's inherited, and there are no known causes or cures, but the skin, its homeostasis, and all cell changes are conscientiously controlled. Inherited diseases are psychosomatically suspected, and when they strike within families, without bacteria or viruses, symptoms indicate they are individually required.

Since inheritance and disease is a vast, confusing mystery, it's more easily believed that noninfectious maladies are shared with and through personalities. Family-member interactions, with similar-disease-acquiring tendencies, where the disease have no known causes or cures, seemingly fortify the belief. This will be detailed more deeply in the following chapters.

10.6 ARTHRITIS

The word arthritis is derived from the Greek word arthron, which means joint. Actually, it now means joint inflammation; the disease affects joints, and its "cures" could outnumber the diseases' incidences. The more common arthritic disease types are rheumatoid, osteoarthritis, and gouty arthritis. Prehistoric man's remains show arthritic signs.

Rheumatoid arthritis, an inflammatory disorder, is the more common one. The synovial-membrane (densely connective tissue) becomes inflamed, and when left untreated, it frequently thickens, and the consequential synovial fluid accumulates; swelling and pain start. Abnormal tissues then develop, which adhere to the articular-cartilage surface. When destroyed, the exposed-joint ends become joined by tissue ossification (bone substance altering). Frequently when one body part, right or left hand, is inflamed the other is also affected.

The primary hand or body part, however, is usually the most severely inflamed. Many patients have both knees affected, while others have both elbows impaired. During intervention therapy, patients' primary hand, elbow or foot always heals last.

Some doctors believe that viruses program arthritic conditions, while others believe that they are accidentally originated; anger, however, is a growing origination cause. When certain personalities harbor intense anger, arthritic formations occur. Intense emotions certainly augment arthritic formations, but they, obviously, are not the cause; they're a consciously exhibited, subconscious formed, and conscientious directed emotional-problem displayed, only. Simply, individuals harbor repressed fears, and the conscience uses arthritic conditions to impede feared compliances; the conditions, although pathologically and painfully dangerous, merely become the physical barriers between patients and their anxieties.

Osteoarthritis is a non-inflammatory, degenerative disease that timely progresses, but usually doesn't cripple the sufferers. It irritates joints through timely wear and tear; however, everyone ages, but not everyone gets osteoarthritis, and the disease develops more readily in some families.

Articular-cartilage degeneration characterizes the disease. The degeneration exposes the joint-bone ends; small bumps or spurs are formed; and new tissue forms on the exposed ends. The restrictive space programs reoccurring pain; however, unlike rheumatoid arthritis, osteoarthritis infrequently fuses because the synovial membrane is seldom destroyed. Regeneration is common and expected in adjusted homeostasis, but it frequently turns to degeneration and arthritis when interfered by strong emotions.

Family formations seemingly augment gouty arthritis. Uric acid, a waste product, unites with sodium and forms a salt, which is excreted in urine. When kidneys no longer sufficiently excrete uric acid, the salts accumulate in soft tissue; kidneys and joints are the typical sites, and are soon injured. When left untreated, the salty crystals destroy the soft tissue, identical to rheumatoid arthritis; after fusing, the joints are unmovable.

Family members frequently develop gouty arthritis, which seemingly augments doctors' inherited beliefs, but the disease is often strengthened by emotional stress; it's more often found within intense families, and it coincides with increased anger. It's simply, consequential stress; if parents have one form, the children will also. Seemingly, when authoritarian-oppressive-parents sternly discipline children, they, too, show increased anger levels and develop the same disease. Observably, when children are disciplined through some method that doesn't utilize parental aggression, children express less anger.

Interestingly, a parent observed children's schoolyard behavior, and then noted students' aggressive behavior toward other children. Afterward, the adult questioned the parents about the discipline used and found that aggressive children were frequently disciplined with corporal punishment, while non-aggressive children came from more adjusted and autonomous, parental relationships.

Anger and its causes obviously program arthritic and other psychosomatic diseases, and most common personality characteristics are found in many arthritic patients. They all have increased, intense anger levels; some hide it, but through emotional outbursts exhibit its extreme nature. The elevated emotion also surfaces through incessant talking, or by extreme uncontrollable nervous body movements.

Children reared by angry parents will always form identical anger harboring personalities. The author's mother carried rheumatoid arthritis to her grave, and the author's siblings exhibit various arthritic forms. Obviously, the conscience largely directs most body activity, and the subconscious harbors strong emotions. Practically, this should be somewhat comforting, for it makes us completely self-accountable.

10.7 MUSCULAR DYSTROPHIES

Muscular Dystrophies are a degenerative disease group that medical experts assume is inherited and is definitely, timely progressive, and doctors have practically no insight into its cures or causes.

After inset, the muscles become enlarged and weakened. The muscular dystrophy Duchenne branch usually affects male children early, as left and right side muscles that support body movement are severally impaired; death is usually programmed very early.

In the muscular-dystrophy-myotonias branch, both sexes are affected, and both body-side muscles are impaired, while internal muscles, frequently the diaphragm, are unaffected.

Patients show poor, faulty potassium-metabolism rates and can't utilize creatine. Some commonly, frequently found, physical irregularities are the following: patients are prematurely bald, emaciated or obese, emotionally unstable, and have atrophied sex glands. The biological symptoms are all conscientiously controlled. Perhaps, its incidence and cure are not beyond psychosomatic explanation.

10.8 MYASTHENIA GRAVIS

Myasthenia Gravis is another disease that attacks the muscles; it usually occurs in females between twenty and fifty years old and is frequently found in skeletal muscles, which progressively weaken and seemingly are caused by neuromuscular-junction malfunctions. The conscience releases ACH which programs muscle activity. In myasthenia gravis, antibodies counteract the ACH, which leaves insufficient quantities to activate additional muscles. Progressively, other junctions are affected, and patients grow weaker. If not treated successfully, it can be fatal.

The conscience controls all muscular diseases. Unfortunately, doctors seemingly read the changes programmed by strong, emotional trauma, only; they must explore the emotional-trauma causes. The disease is certainly portrayed by individuals who are not emotionally comfortable, and the symptoms merely reflect inner conflicts. A complete new medical approach is absolutely necessary.

10.9 PARKINSON DISEASE

Parkinson's disease is a progressive, degenerative sickness that exhibits strong skeleton muscular movements. Seemingly, it's centered in the cerebrum's basal ganglia; it attacks the neurons that release the exciter-transmitter dopamine. The symptoms include involuntary and uncontrolled skeletal movements, excessive hand tremors, awkward walking, and facial-tissue rigidity; the victims will frequently have open mouths and drool saliva with their clumsy body movements. Their walking is restricted; they lurch and hunch forward, and their hands are frequently drawn and twisted grotesquely. Although patients feel touchingly warm, their blood pressures are frequently low. The idiopathic section, visualized by spontaneous symptoms, is the more common.

Startlingly, patients with the disease frequently develop cancer, tuberculosis, multiple sclerosis, or cold infections far below the average, and when an infection develops, antibodies are successful and linger in bodies abnormally long; tranquilizing drugs seemingly help the patients. Younger patients sometimes have surgery, but the symptoms usually return.

Some doctors believe that premature aging and nerve cell deaths are the primary causes of the disease. But, the malady must be psychosomatically induced because the grotesquely, consciously displayed symptoms (including the antibody retentions) are conscientiously controlled.

10.10 CEREBRAL PALSY

Doctors think that cerebral palsy is a motor disorder group that perhaps is programmed by motor-brain damage, which could be caused during pregnancy, birth, or infancy; doctors additionally believe that pregnant mothers could program the disease. Developing-expectant mothers, sometimes, contact German measles and damage three brain parts: the cortex, the cerebrum's basal ganglia, and the cerebellum.

Some doctors believe that could be one causative factor, but all cerebral-palsy-patients' mothers didn't develop measles during pregnancy, and the disease causing pathological-body movements are all conscientiously controlled. Conclusively, some palsy patients have been psychotherapeutically treated and were completely, symptomatically relieved.

10.11 MULTIPLE SCLEROSIS

Sclerosis, a Greek word, means hard. In multiple sclerosis, the central-nervous-system deteriorates; the neurons of the myelin sheaths harden, and the neuroglia cells that support neurons an produce myelin sheaths around neuron axons are damaged or disappear. Seemingly, the stair shaped cells proliferate, and scleroses begin; the sheaths, enclosing the axons, harden. Cortexes, the reasoning brain parts, transmit and receive messages through the myelin sheaths, but scleroses' rapid progression interfere with neurons' impulse transmissions.

Several-major early disease's symptoms are poor hand co-ordinations and progressive penmanship impairments. Additionally, corticospinal tract short-circuits program paralysis of the leg muscles, double vision and urinary tract infections, which usually fade, reappear; numbness, then sets in.

Unfortunately, the disease's progression programs muscle-control loss and eventually ambulation impairments. Death, in seven to thirty years, which is frequently programmed through urinary infections, usually follows the incident of the original symptoms.

Doctors believe that viral infections program autoimmune responses; the viruses program neuroglial cells and the immune systems' antibody destructions. But, the subconscious programs the functions, and the conscience directs them; when the patients' immune system fights their bodies, the disease portrays angry personalities fighting themselves.

Amyotrophic lateral sclerosis (Lou Gehrig's disease) is a brain and spinal cord progressive disorder, which usually affects arm and leg muscles first. The disease weakens the hands and programs arms and legs irregular jerking. The frequent treatment, electric shock, supposedly, forcibly programs the body to fight against the disease. Other treatment methods, immunosuppressive therapy (drugs that stop patients' immunization processes), and spinal cord electrical stimulation are indeed questionable.

The disease's symptoms and consequential treatments imply strong, pathological psychosomatic connections. The immunity systems' malfunctions, only, strengthen the belief; the body, independently, has no organ that can direct the simultaneously various biological irregularities.

10.12 CYSTIC FIBROSIS

Cystic Fibrosis is an exocrine glandular disease; it disrupts the functions of the pancreas, salivary, sweat glands, and respiratory systems. Its more common symptoms are pancreatic dysfunctions and liver cirrhosis; it frequently programs thick exocrine mucus (a non-drainable buildup in the respiratory system) and infections are programmed. Also, pancreatic juice is interrupted, which prevents normal digestion. The fatty foods' non-digestions program vitamin A, D and K deficiencies. Thereby, children-patients are administered pancreatic juices and large doses of the vitamins.

10.13 PSYCHO MOTOR EPILEPSY

Epilepsy programs patient abnormal-pathological behavior. The medical-professionals' have many and varied diseases-originative explanations, which are the following: various head injuries, tumors, brain abscesses, various children's infections, and other unexplained reasons, called idiopathic.

Probably, some childhood infections did injure some young patients, but not all childhood trauma sufferers, similarly inflicted, develop epilepsy. Then, the real causes are somewhat obscured.

Revealingly, the attacks, preceded by emotional trauma, program pathological, psychosomatic behaviors, and dissipate quickly.

Actually, their psychosomatic linkage is believable because many epileptics (grand mal, petite mal, and psychomotor) have been treated successfully with intervention therapy; it's strange that patients continue seeking nonexistent medical cures.

10.14 CEREBROVASCULAR ACCIDENTS

Blood-brain-supply interruptions program cerebrovascular accidents (frequently called strokes or cerebral apoplexies). The infarction-groups program intra-cerebral hemorrhaging, cerebral-arteries' atherosclerosis, aneurysms, and embolisms. An embolism is an air bubble, blood clot or any foreign particle that restricts the blood passage to the brain's pia mater. Unfortunately, atheroscleroses (plaque-formations, within the arteries' lumens, block and restrict both blood and glucose passages, and also program brain damages.

All cardiovascular functions are conscientiously, controlled, as heart patients most frequently show intense anger, rage and anxiety. Alarmingly, many patients are pre-heart-attack warned (by prolonged angina pain), and do nothing.

The conscience, combined with intense anxieties, is compelled to act; heart attacks are the frequently required outcome. The entire predictable process portrays imperfect personalities working within perfect bodies, and it's simply individualistic; the sole responsibility remains personal and painful, but avoidable.

The author observed two friends who developed pending heart-irregularity symptoms, and they were informed, did nothing, and both proceeded to their destiny, twelve to twenty-four months later. The attack signals, emotional behavior and physical abnormalities, made the future circulatory and heart problems easily predictable.

10.15 HEART DISEASE

Mostly, heart diseases are defined as coronary artery diseases, and called C.A.D., which is a complex group that develops slowly and usually requires years of non-detection; the statistics are staggering. Nationally, heart diseases program over 500,000 deaths annually; over 300,000 are sudden deaths. Over 800,000 people are admitted to hospitals annually, and the medical profession hasn't a disease-originative clue, due to poor information, indifference or greed.

Since heart illnesses are mostly major artery disorders, they are divided into several categories: congenital, hypertension, and coronary heart disease.

Congenital heart disease usually starts before birth. The problems seemingly begin embryonally; many heart malformations assumingly are programmed by pre-birth infections, prenatal nutritional deficiencies, and pregnant mothers alcohol consumption and tobacco use. Other harmful drug uses are a causative factor. Now, some doctors feel that some mothers are more prone to have maldeveloped babies. Unfortunately, psychosomatic problems are never considered; factually, not all mothers want or expect pregnancies, and the babies are frequently unwelcome. Additionally, the future babies face unhappy homes, unfriendly and unmarried parents; prenatal heart mal-formations are almost predictable.

Unfortunately, both parents' strong emotions also affect the embryo. For instance, an unhappy couple, acquaintances of the author, produced two almost identical premature boys, two years apart. They both were born with undeveloped hearts and lungs, and required approximately six months incubations before deaths. Both parents' strong emotions, and continual drug use, seemingly, interplayed into the boys' premature births and undeveloped organs.

Rheumatic heart disease is an inflammable disorder involving the heart and surrounding muscles, due to rheumatic fever.

Arterial-lumens' restrictions, pathologically programmed, produce diseased and damaged hearts.

Predictably, future heart patients are easily profiled. They are highly neurotic overweight, less physically active, smoke nicotine, and drink alcohol excessively. They are highly competitive and frequently, excessively consume coffee. Consequently, many doctors now connect elevated stress and nicotine consumption with heart attacks. The physically over-developed male, before age forty, is a likely heart attack candidate. Some doctors use the word, predestination, and frequently blame one tiny male semen cell. Actually, the heart is only a pump, but literature and songs have portrayed it differently.

Heart trouble usually encompasses the entire blood-circulatory system. Since heart problems are mostly circulatory problems, they are easily divided into two common forms: arteriosclerosis and atherosclerosis.

Although they are the more common types, they are not the only two. The latter, atherosclerosis, is the more common one; it's commonly identified when fatty substances (cholesterol) accumulate, harden and restrict arterial-inner surfaces. Several factors enhance the developments: high blood pressure, carbon-monoxide gas (cigarette smoking), and high cholesterol blood levels.

Plateletes (colorless blood cells) collect and adhere to arterial lumens; some doctors seemingly believe that atherosclerosis develops where smooth-muscle cells have been injured. The platelets, then, release clot-forming chemicals, and smooth muscle cells absorb the cholesterol on artery-walls called, tunica media. The atherosclerotic plaque increases and obstructs blood passage; perhaps the rough surfaces program future-blood-clot formations, and a thrombus is formed. The clot can separate and form an embolus, which can obstruct small arteries, capillaries and veins.

Observably, some individuals develop heart problems earlier and more seriously than others; doctors call them heart-problem tendencies, heredity or predestinations.

10.16 HYPERTENSION

Hypertension means high blood pressure but is largely inaccurate. Hyper means up, or increased; tension means to be tense or nervous. Our English-speaking forefathers knew more about high blood pressure causes than present doctors.

The pressure is merely a medical reading that indicates a programmed inner tension, and it's also a disease that includes about one in five individuals, which affects the blood system, heart, brain, and kidneys.

It is measured on a blood-pressure gauge, which almost anyone can read. The two readings indicate arterial pressure while the heart is pumping and while the heart is between beatings. The highest reading, heart-pumping, is called systolic; the lower is called diastolic or heart-resting. A pressure reading of 120 over 80 is called normal, while 140 over 90 is called hypertensive; above is called dangerously hypertensive. About 85 or 90% of hypertensive cases fall into a class called primary hypertension; it occurs if doctors can't find a medical-disease explanation. With the remaining 15% doctors find a medical reason, which is called secondary hypertension. The biological reasons are kidney problems, atheroscleroses, and adrenal hyper-secretions.

Atherosclerosis, is a progressive disease that restricts the blood flow to the kidneys and other organs. The resultant, restrictive blood flow and nutrient reductions, program the kidneys to release rennin into the blood, which catalyzes the strong blood-vessel-constrictor formation called angiotensin 11, which programs blood pressure elevations and vessel-wall constrictions. The elevated pressure thickens the kidney walls and further elevates the blood pressure. The constrictions of the vessel walls narrow the arterial lumen and vein passages, which further elevates the blood pressure.

The last biological hypertension section is well named. Although inner intensive danger is well known, many people still die annually from its presence.

Arteriosclerosis, arterial-wall hardening (elasticity loss) and the increased blood supply demands, programs systolic pressure increases.

The diastolic pressure is taken while the heart is relaxing; an elevation implies that there is some arterial restrictions or the narrowing of the arterioles' lumen. An elevated diastolic reading is the more dangerous because progressive hypertension programs increased atherosclerosis and artheriosclerosis' growths, which program myocardial infarctions or heart deaths.

Heart patients, medical professionally profiled, are genetically hypertensive, obese, smoke, and they all must be tense, but they don't show the neurosis identically. Hereditarily, individuals can be predestined when they are born and raised by severely intense parents; if one parent has hypertension, 50% of the children will be similarly diseased. If both parents have the problem, 90% of the children will develop high blood pressure.

10.17 HEART FAILURE

Heart failure, which is variously programmed, is characterized by an insufficient blood and oxygen supply. A decreased oxygenized blood supply to the heart programs infarctions or muscle deaths. And both atherosclerosis and arteriosclerosis often program heart failures; many patents show both related diseases.

Heart failures can develop on either heart side, probably demanded by various personalities; obviously, a prolonged oxygenated blood shortage weakens the heart and programs heart failures, which in turn orchestrate various-organ-blood accumulations.

10.18 BLOOD CLOTTING OR THROMBOSIS

Plaque commonly forms within artery's lumens. As the resultant atheroscleroses progress, it will frequently break free and form blood clots, which will eventually block blood passages. The condition is called thromboses, or the artery is thrombosed, and the resultant inflammation frequently programs other thrombosed vessels.

10.19 STROKES (CEREBRAL VASCULAR ACCIDENTS)

Strokes or cerebral-vascular accidents occur when there is an interruption of blood to the brain. Blood clots, compressions, spasms, and arterial constrictions program the disease. Arterial blockings (atherosclerotic-growth separations) are the more common; they frequently cause brain damage.

An artery rupture, a stroke, which deprives the brain of blood, frequently happens deep within the brain; prolonged hypertension is most frequently the culprit.

10.20 ANEURYSMS

Aneurysms, (blood filled sacs, formed on any major arterial walls) are dangerous; high blood pressure, frequently, precedes the growths. Bursting within brains, they cause strokes and deaths. Additionally, when arterial walls weaken, aneurysms form, which are conscientiously programmed. Their originations are quite simple: childhood or adult repressions equate tension; aneurysms and other vascular circulatory problems that affect the heart are the result.

July the fourth, 2004, the author was diagnosed to have a four centimeter digestive aneurysm. Recognizing its psychosomatic significance, the author immediately worked in therapy. Three months later an C.T. scan showed it had grown to four and half centimeters. Figuring that multiple repressions must have programmed its origination and growth, the author then proceeded to work in therapy twice a week for six months. The following C.T. scan showed that it's size had been reduced to one and seven tenths centimeters. A year later, after more work in therapy whereby the author recalled many childhood repressions involving parental aggressions, a C.T. scan showed that the aneurysm was gone. Within the author's knowledge, it has never been done before.

10.21 CORONARY ARTERY SPASMS

Coronary artery spasms, the sudden smooth heart muscle contractions, program vasoconstrictions, with or without atherosclerosis, and produce heart attacks and, often, sudden deaths.

10.22 ARRHYTHMIAS

Arrhythmias, irregular heartbeats, program many deaths; often, patients don't reach the hospital alive. Strong emotions interrupt the heart-impulse-conduction-system; biologically, they're called heart blocks. Other less-deadly irregular heartbeats are called flutters and fibrillations, which can often be medically controlled.

The entire heart disease coverage, obviously, hasn't been accomplished or tried, but a familiar term, psychosomatic, re-emerges. It's still misunderstood and frightens many individuals; however, the heart is energized through the vagus nerves, and various secreted body chemicals, which are conscientiously directed. Another word re-emerges, hypertension; repressed fears cause hypertensions, and the conscientiously programmed anxieties produce the personally required heart problems.

Again, heart patients are heavy smokers, highly ambitious, and overweight, who frequently have family histories of heart disease. The personality-displays are merely neurotic conscious behaviors, but are subconsciously, emotionally born. The strong emotion, anger, again is found. The medical profession believing that the body acts independently often prevents any subconscious, conscience duel causative knowledge, and much money is made while treating the body separately. Factually, most, if not all, heart problems are psychosomatic. The medical profession must study patients' personalities, their hearts and their entire bodies. The public knowledge that myocardial infarctions frequently program sudden deaths, change lives, and destroy patients' bank accounts hasn't reduced heart attack incidences; they have increase. The desired changes must include more than just medically administered drug applications and often, useless, health advice.

Treating heart disease, cardiovascular doctors frequently perform bypass heart surgeries. Shortly after successful surgery, many patients unexpectedly and unexplainably die. The doctors then found that the arteries' bypass sections had simply constricted and stopped the bloods' flow. In other deaths, doctors found that plaque formations stopped the blood's flow. Unfortunately, doctors ignore personalities existing within bodies, and the strong emotions existing within the subconscious. They ignore the vagus nerve transmissions, and the consciously exhibited, subconsciously born, anxiety observances. Since hypertension and cardiovascular problems are, all too frequently, connected, deaths are predictable.

10.23 PEPTIC ULCERS

Ulcers are crater lesions, formed within membranes. Within the alimentary canal, they are exposed to gastric juice and called peptic ulcers. Found in the stomach, they are called gastric ulcers; in the duodenal, they called duodenal ulcers.

Doctors feel that they have three causes: an over secretion of gastric-acids, strong emotions, and vagus nerve over stimulations. The ulcer explanations are redundant because the vagus nerves, conscientiously directed, drive the entire process. Ulcer patients have inferiority complexes, which program inner tensions, and the vital nerves merely transmit tense messages; gastric juices are increased and ulcers are formed.

They can be very serious because, when tensions persist, gastric acids can eat through the alimentary-tract lining. The resultant perforations cause bleedings, which frequently promote peritonitis. That is an acute inflammation of the abdominal-cavity. It frequently leads to deaths.

Strong emotions frequently interfere with normal digestive activity. Babies, too, have alimentary tract ulcers. The answers are simple; ulcers are consciously felt, but conscientiously programmed through subconsciously repressed fears.

Birth starts the conscious, but evidence shows that the subconscious and conscience pre-exists births. Observed embryos frequently show stressful signs (one male embryo exhibited an erection), and frequently, children and adults remember their mother's enduring-prenatal-emotional experiences. When expectant mothers harbor strong emotions, the carried embryos frequently show stressful signs. And finally, reincarnations beliefs are not anti-Christian.

10.24 OBESITY

Perhaps obesity isn't a true disease, but it frequently programs diseases and deaths. It seemingly follows affluence; its presence always signifies that the sufferer is angry.

Individuals who weigh fifteen percent or more than an accepted standard are considered obese, and medical doctors state its causes are the following: regulatory and metabolic. The first is much more commonly found; it occurs when personalities overeat. The reasons are the following: neurotic overeating, aging, poor exertion, and decreased need for digestive calories (metabolic-dysfunctional need). All four are psychosomatic; if aging alone caused obesity, all elderly people would be overweight. The metabolic problems (the catabolic reduction of carbohydrates and fats) are typically blamed. Thyroxin-hypo-secretion is one example.

When obesity continues, doctors attack it along several lines. First, they, seeking organic explanations, perform several tests. Then patients are strictly dieted. When dieting proves unsuccessful, doctors explain three operations: intestinal bypass, gastric stapling, and gastric banding.

The first explained operation creates a bypass, which attaches the jejunum to the lower ileum. It essentially eliminates many small-intestine-absorptive surfaces, and digestive vitamins and nutrients are reduced. That could be important when individuals age and experience declining-food appetites.

An upper stomach, limiting pouch, stapling procedure simply, drastically restricts patients' digestion space. Reinforced orifices restrict the stomachs' absorption abilities. Unfortunately, it's frequently dangerous and unsuccessful because after surgery, patients must live with un-addressed, pathologically enlarged appetites. Gastroplasty has simply limited the capacity; patients frequently overeat, spend more time ingesting and regurgitating, and they adjust and frequently regain the lost weight.

Nylon cords (gastric bandings) that form stomach-limiting pouches are the safest, if any are safe. Unfortunately, all three are frequently unsuccessful because they ignore obesity's prominent cause. They are mostly performed through lack of knowledge and greed; the surgeries program many dangerous side effects: the limited absorption process eventually programs vitamin and nutrient deficiencies, and when weights are regained, patients frequently are depressed; the strong emotions, which triggered the enlarged appetites, were completely ignored. The unattended emotional problems continually enlarge, and eventually cause drastic, patient changes.

The author knew an obese family who were also wealthy. Three brothers and a nephew each tried the gastroplasty process; all failed. They each regurgitated food following surgery, and later, they all, through lengthened eating habits, mostly regained the original weights.

Continual corpulence (programmed by anger, rage and anxiety) left unchecked, program many physical problems, perhaps hypertension, and other cardiovascular disease. Unfortunately, sudden deaths frequently occur because obesity and premature deaths are connected. Since all appetites are conscientiously controlled and directed, all obesity must be psychosomatic. Obesity and diseases are constant companions, and most diseases must be, not only conscientiously connected, but also directed. Since personal nutritional needs are almost completely controlled conscientiously; conscious only efforts to reduce food ingestions will usually fail.

10.25 DIABETES MELLITUS

Diabetes Mellitus affects the carbohydrate metabolism. With the disease, the insulin production is reduced, stopped, or the body's insulin sensitivity is affected. The pancreas' endocrine section (the cells cluster called, islets of langerhans) frequently shows early signs. Within it is found three body cell types: first, the alpha cells, which produce the hormone glucagons. Second, the beta cells, which produce the hormone insulin, and third, the delta cells, which produce the growth hormone inhibiting factor (GHIf). Additionally, it's called somatostatin and inhibits insulin production.

Diabetes is a complex disease group, which ultimately alters the production of, or hinders the body's sensitivity to insulin, and blood glucose elevations are effected.

The disease has two major divisions: the first is the adult or maturity type, which usually starts after patients are forty years old or older. The second is the juvenile type, which usually develops while patients are children. The diabetes-maturity-section numbers comprise approximately ninety percent of the total patients, and dieting usually controls the disease. Many diabetic patients produce insulin sufficiently, but the insulin attacks its target cells, and the body's insulin-machineries pathologically malfunction. The juvenile group, much smaller numerically, is more severe initially. Measles, mumps, or other virus infections frequently precede the second type. The younger patient type is characterized by numerous, large, pancreas beta cells that program blood-insulin insufficiencies, which produce blood-glucose elevations. It's frequently called the insulin-dependent diabetes.

The insulin-reductions program a breakdown of reserve fat, which promotes ketosis (organic acid's over productions), which lowers the blood's Ph and can cause deaths.

The initial symptoms are the following: increased urinary volume, hunger, thirst, itching, weakness, and weight loss.

Objectively, doctors limit the quantities of glucose-blood; insulin is injected, and patients are strictly dieted (limiting the ingestions of carbohydrates and fats) to maintain and enforce normal body weights. When patients diet unsuccessfully, lipids invade body cells, and are often deposited on arteries' lumens. Atherosclerosis, and many other cardiovascular problems increase and cause deaths.

The diabetic complex is much greater than this simple description. Additionally, doctors don't know the diseases' causes or cures. The various types seemingly have some genetic connections, and also have some environmental and psychological explanations.

10.26 INFECTIOUS DISEASES

The infectious diseases' grouping is divided into two groups: germ induced and virus induced, and both groups program many diseases. Medical doctors treat the multi-symptoms accurately; however they again fail to recognize conscience directions. Simply, mostly, living or dying, being physically healthy, or disease burdened, is a subconsciously born, conscientiously directed decision.

10.27 ACQUIRED IMMUNITY DEFICIENCY SYNDROME

AIDS destroy the bodies' immune systems. Early symptoms include the following: severe weight loss, fever, weakness, and enlarged lymph glands. Two viruses, closely related, infect the T-lymphocytes (an important immune system component). The de-

veloping disease produces organic infections that frequently program deaths. AIDS patients also frequently develop rare cancers
(lymphomas and carcinomas, squamous-cell malignancies).

Individuals, after exposure, keep the AIDS virus within, and
after several years, without proper medical treatment, they then
develop the disease. The scenario indicates that the subconscious,
(conscience) plays a vital part in the acquiring and developing of
the disease. Simply, when fears and anxieties are harbored, deadly
diseases are developed. Some individuals are sick constantly, while
others never get sick. Strong emotions force the conscience to
shield the personality. For instance, the elderly, repress, harbor, and
intensify anxieties, and are accordingly more sickly with many diseases.

Universally, every one is generally exposed to almost identical
diseases, but don't develop them equally. The mysterious answers
to why must be within the subconscious and conscience. The medical profession states that the answers lie within the individual's
disease resistance, but even that is affected by strong emotions and
neuroses. The answer lies within personalities. Although animal
life repressions have existed since time's beginning, their causes
have remained unchanged. Basically, all animals repress fears, harbor them, develop personalities and consequently display the abnormalities. The various repressed fears are never numerically limited, and the animal mind, mostly human, has severely diversified
and conscientiously enforced the dire results.

Realistically even children exercise conscience selectivity, but
adult more frequently use it very drastically. Therefore, through
fear repressions, personalities are formed, subconsciously housed,
and progressively developed. Then developed personalities (conscientiously selected and enforced) program various diseases and
illnesses.

It's doubtful that children or adults reach dangerous emotional
mental positions without many emotional-subconsciously and con-

scientiously enforced danger signals having been felt and consciously recognized. Adults, frequently, disregard them while following their conscientiously forced, consciously chosen life-styles, thereby using the many associated-anxiety-avoidance behaviors. Children frequently display help wanted signals, which parents and other adults ignore and discourage through lack of knowledge and self-protective adult and parental fears. School-authoritative personnel frequently ignore the same help wanted signals through the same poor defense methods.

Then progressively, from the developed personalities (largely influenced through repressions and the evolving and strengthening anxieties), consciences direct body changes, accidents, and disease. The consequences are shown and felt consciously, but all survival instincts must originate subconsciously. Fortunately, the before mentioned information is good news, for it portrays that life is not hopeless.

Chapter Eleven

The Subconscious Mind and Deaths

It took years before the author could accept that death was largely a subconsciously born, conscientiously programmed mental and physical condition.

Yet, personalities, informingly, must have a clear idea of what the word means. Death has many different meanings; religions and faiths fear the concept, and it seemingly fills the thoughts of many individuals, yet its meanings have timely changed. In early biblical times, death included the ending of existences, forever. Abraham felt that his next life must be lived vicariously through his sons and future generations.

Many modern individuals frequently view it as a physical-life's removal, and a spiritual-life's gain. Some religions teach that its believers take their physical bodies intact beyond deaths. Thereby deaths merely become escape mechanisms, as anxiety free lives beckon beyond the grave.

Now, deaths have taken greater meanings because medical science can remove vital organs from recently departed individuals and transfer them to ill patients. Since normal behavior was bent and broken regarding the transfer of vital organs, sanity and comfort demanded that firm rules and laws be passed pertaining to deaths.

Accordingly, over-time, total-brain inactivity means death, and it's recognized if individuals are not breathing or have no heart activities. The questions then arise, why? Why does everyone die?

Some of the answers are anger; anger-filled violence's capacitate emergency rooms. With ages fifteen to twenty-five, over sixty-five percent of deaths are programmed by accidents, homicides, and suicides.

Anger and rage program most murders and suicides, and suicidal patients clearly show depressions, programmed by repressions and personally directed anger. Highway auto accidents are easily categorized because over fifty percent are alcohol related. Over twenty-two percent of home accidents are connected to alcohol. Our nation alcoholically leads the world. Alcoholics, after dependency, live about twelve years. Many dependant, maladjusted personalities, accompanied by malnutrition, die from programmed diseases; other commit depression-programmed suicides. Alcohol is a depressant; it and depression form a deadly partnership, and strong emotions combined with any drug-use are always dangerous.

Accident victims liter highways; they're placed there through alcohol use, other drug use, simple carelessness, almost nonexistent highway courtesy, impatience (a common neurotic sign), and many other apparent accidental symptoms. Anger and anxiety are commonly found throughout the accident scene.

Generally, every one has a seventy percent chance of dying by accidents, heart disease, homicides, and suicides; modern medicine hasn't changed the figures.

It's found that anger and hypertensions' high readings are frequently combined; rage and resentment are often present. When hypertensive readings reached 160/100 or higher, aggression, anxiety, depression, and guilt are frequently found. There is, also, a positive correlation between intense emotions and neoplastic (cancerous tumor) growths.

Born today, one of two babies will die from cardiovascular renal disease. Overall, 70% will die from accidents, neoplasms, heart diseases, homicides and suicides.

Although universally found, anger isn't the killer; it's only the consciously exhibited correlation with the cause, and it's the personality connections with maladjustments, strife, disease, and deaths.

Anger, born within the subconscious, is always found with unhappy individuals, who are actually fighting themselves. Unfortunately the programmed diseases and deaths are, most frequently, conscientiously programmed.

11.1 SUICIDES

Obviously, suicidal personalities, timely methodically plan their deaths; the subconscious-conscientious connections are obvious. They have subconsciously born poor self-esteems; the consequently exhibited, inferiority complexes, programmed by repressed fears, mandate the unworthy feelings. The accompanying guilt, which they all show, is also directed by the conscience.

Inferiority complexes frequently program the following feelings and thoughts: being unclean, unworthy, inferior, guilty, deserving punishment, deserving sicknesses, deserving deaths, unloved, and have employment and unemployment nightmares. Entirely, the complexes and depression strongly correlate.

The potentially suicidal individuals are hyperactive and adjust poorly; they frequently show intense anger. Being obviously discontented and uncomfortable, suicide is frequently threatened, and the conscious lives merely reflect subconsciously born anger, rage, and anxiety. Since all three are found in all suicidal personalities, and every one universally, somewhat, harbors them, then maybe everyone is, slightly, suicidal.

Depressed personalities need therapy immediately, and need family-activity participations; successful-event activities are always helpful. They must be shown that they are needed, loved, and where possible, separated from alcohol and other drugs.

11.2 ACCIDENTS

True, totally complete accidental accidents are very rare because angry and self-destructive personalities frequently program many wrecks. Death defying, reckless drivers seemingly, deliberately program many of them; highly neurotic, self-destructive individuals are angry and frequently sexually insecure. Factually, personalities, both sexes, who are maladjusted, frequently, drive recklessly and aggressively. Their behaviorisms portray impatience, probably the leading highway-accidence-death cause. Unfortunately sexual insecurities and anger are emotional, pathological byproducts. Fear repressions orchestrate consciously shown anger, rage, and anxiety, and frequently force conscious exhibits of sexual insecurities; many one-car incidences, combined with drugs, are probably more suicidal than accidental.

Highway drinking and driving combined with speeding are never accidental, and alcohol consumption combined with suicidal personalities program many highway deaths. The subconscious and conscience play a vital part because personalities are overreacting to inadequacy feelings centered on sexual identities. After drinking or while actually drunk, their minds frequently tell them that they are better drivers. Those facts, combined with autos and speed, promote painful injuries and deaths. All are subconsciously born through fear repressions.

11.3 OBESITY

Obesity is not a proper disease, but programs many, and thereby it becomes a major topic; most societies prominently display it. Affluent individuals, seemingly, are more obesity affected.

Its two divisions are regulatory and metabolic. Regulatory is simply neurotic overeating; the metabolic division has organic linkage. Neurotic overeating is programmed within the subconscious and directed conscientiously. Metabolic metabolism, too, is subconsciously programmed and conscientiously demanded. Strong emotions augment normal hunger, thirst, and sex urges, and thereby promote obesity, sex diversion, and drug use. Through increased metabolic rates, and emotional deviations, common obesity is born. The conscience has simply chosen one, or all, as an anxiety shield. When left untreated, the consequences are severe; when medically treated only, nothing has been solved, and the results frequently remain unaltered.

If an obesity cure is devised, it must deal with the subconscious (the strong emotion's harbor) and the conscience that promotes corpulence. Over-eating has always signified strong emotions, directed by neuroses and elevated anxieties. It simply becomes an anxiety shield. The hypothalamus stores the natural needs for food consumption, thirst, and sex; unfortunately, it also houses all repressions and emotions. The conscience, seated there, also regulates body heat, blood pressure, and all other emotional needs or desires. Understandingly then, strong emotions, (anger, rage and anxiety) frequently program food, sex and thirst abuses; conscious behaviors simply exhibit subconsciously born neurotic, pathological appetites.

Obesities' causes and consequences are well known, yet personalities willingly continue living within its life-style. Then, the expected deaths are almost suicidal, and it's certainly a linkage between the conscience and death. Timely programming, the disease, and the orchestrated, consequential deaths obscure the obvious connections; therefore personalities, overlooking the obvious, are simply living within a chosen life-style, and have programmed their own death patterns.

For each emotion there is a corresponding subconscious to conscience reason. Strong emotions, consequently, follow repressed fears. Neuroses are naturally, pathologically developed; increased anxieties augment them, and strong unrealistic life-styles are programmed to reduce the elevated anxieties. Diseases consequently follow, and programmed deaths emerge; but before deaths, some life-styles alter minds (promote rigidity) and impede most, if not all positive emotional adjustments. Image altering (body changes) and other pathological life-styles frequently bring on excessive food and drug use. Those too are frequently found with suicidal patients.

11.4 MYOCARDIAL INFARCTIONS

Provably, all cardiovascular problems are subconsciously formed, conscientiously directed; continual repressions frequently require cardiovascular problems. The orchestrated inner tension (hypertension) eventually will always negatively impact healthy homeostasis.

The neurotic and highly neurotic personalities involved, simply, necessitate personally selected cardiovascular problems; time and tension program the organic damages, and deaths soon follow. The consciences, purposefully, but direly, alleviate the raging anxiety through deaths.

The author had a friend who suffered a heart attack several years ago. The friend was approached and his condition was discussed. He stated that the attack was serious; it had damaged his heart, and the medical treatments were mostly worthless. He was then reminded that there was a curable method; after questioning the author about the treatment, he stated, "I would rather die than enter therapy and work within the subconscious mind."

That individual, a self-made millionaire, chose a terrible painful death rather than a painless cure. His repressions, developed fears and anxieties, programmed his life-styles and mental rigidity; he personally selected and programmed his death. Many intelligent individuals choose pathological life-styles, and remain within them, steadfastly, throughout life.

The author had another friend who was hypertensive; raised by hypertensive parents, he showed early disease symptoms. Approached by the friend, the author offered his services freely. Not surprisingly, the offer was refused, yet it was obvious that the friend, who was 56, without therapeutic intervention, would not reach 60; six months later the friend was found dead. The dear person chose death rather than consciously recall repressed childhood repressions. The unknown adjustment fears were largely hidden beneath the formed-life-style living, and the conscientiously directed, subconsciously stored anxiety.

11.5 MALIGNANCIES

The connection between malignancy and death is clearly established, and its emotional connection is also well known. Since every cell growth and division are directed by either the pituitary gland or by various chemicals, which the medical profession believes, there still must be either conscious or conscientious mental directions. Strong emotions and increasing anxieties frequently disrupt normal-cell divisions; personalities, and the anxieties' intensifications program the disease. Intensified and augmented anxieties will ultimately hasten the diseases' developments, and probably program the diseases' various body locations.

Some unfortunate sufferers seemingly seek deaths, and often state that they deserve to die; intense anger is profiled. Rapid malignant growths and intense anger are correlated. Some patients mask it and adopt an attitude of "La belle indifference," which seemingly shields the personality.

Initial repressions predate all diseases, and additional repressions augment the subconsciously formed anxieties; the threatened personalities program the diseases, and deaths soon follow. That also explains why the elderly are more sickly and accident-prone; their anxieties augment with time and multiple repressions.

Three terms are positively connected: psychosomatic diseases, strong emotions, and deaths. Since personalities universally harbor strong emotions, they are easily ignored, and the death connections are more acceptably difficult. The brainwashed medical profession helps the concept by constantly publishing latest discoveries that will ultimately cure most diseases. The implication is that bodies can successfully be treated independently; a miracle drug will cure all.

Many individuals think that good health and positive thoughts are correlated, but conscious-resolve, combined with neurosis, only increases inner tensions. Concentration never aids ulcer's healing and it doesn't alter cancers' growths. Unfortunately, time and strong emotions are poorly coordinated, for sickness is never foreign. Its developments seemingly have several factors: repressive repetitions, and strong-emotional developments; combined, they have alarming effects. Then personalities and environmental developments must be factored; perhaps the defense mechanisms that are used throughout life also help the disease developments and ultimately promote deaths. The medical profession simply groups everything into one group called heredity. Unfortunately, sickness and death are strongly coordinated; personalities, mostly, compute selected deaths: mentally ill patients and extremely mal-adjusted individuals have a more shortened-life expectation than well-adjusted ones. For instance alcoholics live about 10 to 20 years, if they continually use alcohol. The only reasonable explanation lies within the subconscious and the conscience. Simply, personalities with healthy self-esteems have more productive and peaceful lives. Obviously life's quality means more than life itself. That thought, but in reverse, seemingly is present with many suicidal personalities because the author has heard several ask, "Why should I live any longer? What do I have to live for?"

Similarly, individuals work, have productive lives, and then die shortly after retirement; extreme anxieties increase, and their consciences simply program escape mechanisms. The ego is protected through death.

Then, the neuroses, sicknesses, and deaths are strongly coordinated. Strong anger, a repressive byproduct, is easily viewable as an emotional maladjustment, and it's frequently, pridefully displayed.

Originally, tuberculosis, a fatal lung disease, was, somewhat, and still is a poor mans' disease. It's frequently found within ghettos and is often combined with smoldering hatred. The disease, early in the world, required rest and proper nourishment, both factors were, somewhat foreign in the ghettos; deaths soon followed. Then maladjustment, sickness and deaths are not only partners, they must be viewed as a cause and effect.

Tuberculosis frequently kills entire families, after starting. That seemingly is more poor thinking rather than a strong disease. The author knew a family where the disease was present who deliberately mistreated their bodies. They actually hastened their own deaths; they drank alcohol and lost sleep, even though they had tuberculosis, and it required complete rest. Emotional maladjustments were apparent, and deaths soon followed; almost the entire family died very young.

Anger, disease, and death underline the pathologically psychosomatic connection; time completes the process.

When people die unattended by doctors, autopsies are usually required; in 2 to 5% of the deaths, the causes are unobtainable, deaths just occurred. Death certificates show that the deceased died from natural causes (what ever that means). Obviously the unexplained deaths were conscientiously directed. Elderly married couples frequently show the same mental development, and then they die almost simultaneously, showing no apparent biological reason.

Family members' "inherited" diseases and deaths tendencies are probably transferred through families' similar personality patterns, rather than within inherited restrictions, for some family members don't develop the disease, and those who do, don't die within a common time frame.

Much evidence virtually proves that most illnesses are conscientiously programmed; thereby anger, rage and consequential illnesses are common partners. Anxieties program the beginnings and augment enlarged inferiority complexes, and subconscious repressions (a required forerunner) direct the growths of the increasing complexes, life-styles selections, inner tension, and deaths.

In viewing deaths and visualizing their subconscious connections, patients' immediate-impending, consciously unsuspected deaths are frequently visualized within conscientiously enforced dreams; they're revealed abstractly. The programmed deaths, of which the author has witnessed several, usually follow within about 12 hours.

Chapter Twelve

Conclusion

Reflectively, obviously, most, if not all, diseases and consequential deaths are subconsciously born, conscientiously directed and programmed, but that creates many problems. Most individuals, including doctors, are uniformed and often even disbelieve that the subconscious exists, and they totally ignore the conscience, although it's a vital part of their minds; they misname and often divinely identify the inner conscience voice and mind which speaks, directs their dreams, and moves various parts of their bodies. The universal belief that the body is independent (at least, where diseases are concerned) is easily accepted. A doctor and friend once told the author that bodies demand food. Obviously, bodies, without minds, make no such demands.

Everyone experiences pain, and death is easily, although falsely, assumed to be consciously, biologically originated. The subconscious and conscience are easily and understandingly ignored; even their existences are disbelieved, and their controls are also often mislabeled. The conscience's death-warnings change nothing, and the deaths are more startling when there are no conscious advanced physical-death warnings. The subconscious and conscience simply, through repressed fears, terrors, and elevated anxieties, necessitate the deaths.

Repressions promote neuroses, and everyone, universally, is neurotic. Without neurosis, perfection would be achieved. A college graduate once stated that she was not neurotic; that view is shared with less educated people, yet it's the neurosis degree and its dire consequences that can really be altered. The alterations (fear reductions through therapy) enhance, lengthen, enrich, and strengthen lives.

Universally, everyone adopts defensive measures to shield a fragile personality; they are as varied as personalities differ. Defining or personal recognition by those individualities is extremely difficult because of living within bodies and having only one personality from which to judge. The place to start is to form some physical and emotional norm for human behavior. This of course must include a common behavioral comfort zone for everyone universally. When that is established every desire, want, and behavior (out side that zone) is pathologically induced.

Some behavioral, adopted pathological signals are shown early, and they soon become biological changes as the anxieties augment. The advanced stages, of course, are more dangerous. They include obesity, excessive weight loss, bowel irregularity, hypertension, rapid foot movement, nonprescription drug use (including alcohol), digestion problems, heart disease, and many if not all other diseases.

All neurotic behavioral problems are programmed by repressions. Simply, personalities chose poor adaptations during traumas, mostly while very young. Unfortunately, the repressed fears, in time. form anxieties, eventually force the forming of emotional barriers, and then enforce the forming of physical barriers. They all either demand the forming of or become the adopted life-styles, and they unsuccessfully strive to shield the personality from anxiety. Eventually the growing anxieties promote various diseases and consequently orchestrate deaths. Before deaths, the emotional barriers and programmed life-styles, centered on the physical barriers, necessitated by strong fears and anxieties, severely lower the quality of life. Obviously, the original repressions augmented by repetitious traumas, consequently program fears, anxieties, strife, lifestyle limitations, disease and deaths.

Personalities, before death, spend much time overcoming self-imposed life-style limitations; they awake daily, fully enthused, but shortly thereafter fail. They adorn the same dark, gloomy, pessimistic outlook. Living within extreme inferiority complexes, they make many decisions poorly. Some fear-enshrouded, life issues can be somewhat realistically visualized, but responses will still be anxiety-hampered.

There are changes that will enrich lives, decrease diseases, and delay deaths: first, children must be taught the word neurotic and its personal meaning. After therapy perhaps, they will recognize abnormal thoughts that arise within everyone. Through that understanding, perhaps normally neurotic individuals would activate fewer aggressive acts; obviously that's a stretch, but there must be some neurotic-thought recognition before many good mental-health-thoughts can surface. Second, human behaviorists must be taught, a bewildering thought, but therapists and counselors, at a leading university, treated subconsciously born neurotic behavioral problems, consciously, only; the subconscious or conscience was totally ignored through lack of knowledge or indifference. Consequently, repressions, fears, and formed anxieties were foreign words.

All personalities who showed abnormal-behavior (including those who exhibited life-style misbehaviors, organic-psychosomatic-physical abnormalities, hand tremors, hair loss, stuttering, homosexuality and other life-style changes) were consciously counseled, only. Desperate-neurotic patients seeking help were told that they should simply, impossibly adjust; a depressed homosexual was told that he would be homosexual for his entire life. Other patients were given the impossible advice that their anxiety filled life-styles were normal, and they must emotionally accept them.

Everyone must recognize that excessive, aggressive ominous thoughts, subconsciously born, are never meaningless. All thoughts and desires have their subconscious births and conscientious connections.

All fears and anxieties are subconsciously born by repressions; only cognizant transfers reduce them. Unfortunately, some past-trauma repressions must be transferred to the conscious because most, if not all, repressed fears are unrealistic to adulthood. The fears are not what was done, but what the victims were afraid that they personally would do. And no thought or repressed fear can equate the consequentially, terrible limiting life-styles, accidents, diseases, and deaths; compared, all consciously revealed repressed fears are totally insignificant. The author frequently laughed following many subconscious to conscious transfers.

Since mostly everyone, universally, thinks almost identical thoughts, and shows the same deep-seated emotions, behaves approximately the same, and eventually retreats into many identical life-styles, the consequently repressions, had to be approximately the same. Personalities program all required individually repressive differences, emotional augmentations, and life-style limitations. Unfortunately, rigid personalities require that some must live within self-established, limiting and frequently diseased life-styles that eventually help program painful and premature deaths.

Also, when emotional problems are timely endured, future generations usually "inherit" them (the consequential diseases are most likely passed on through personality patterns; accordingly, children and grandchildren can suffer the same diseases that limit many individuals, such as: asthma, hay fever, heart problems, and many other limiting and fatal diseases.

The solutions are simple, but frightening: personalities must control their own lives, but taking complete authority requires much sole searching. Being, somewhat, completely in charge, lives and destines are programmed individually. Unfortunately, the orchestration is done through subconsciously centered strong emotions rather than by conscious reasoning or planning because with timely repressions, the conscience becomes an enemy rather than a friend.

The solution, again, is called intervention therapy. Simply, by whatever means, it transfers subconsciously stored fears to the conscious, and the following are reduced or eliminated: fears, anxieties, disease tendencies, strong emotional barriers, and restrictive and limiting (frequently deadly) life-styles. Thereby lives are enriched and joyfully extended.

Following successful therapy (frequently a delightful, lifetime endeavor), personalities are wonderfully changed; they become more peaceful, relaxed, emotionally adjusted, and content. Understandingly, the strong linkage between neuroses and diseases diminish or disappear, and family-inherited diseases frequently vanish forever. Reflectively, entire societies need the same help if male and female children are not safe outside their own homes; adult females are not safe after dark; driving is not safe between 1AM and 2AM, on any given Saturday or Sunday (because of drunk drivers); violence makes any driving dangerous; and many individuals are incarcerated and institutionalized (largely because of repressed fears).

And, it's the author's view, if everyone was well adjusted (strong emotions free), governments would function more efficiently, schools would educate much better; hospitals would be less in demand; jails and penitentiaries would not be as full; mental institutions would not be as needed; accidents would decrease; diseases would be increasingly more infrequent and far less painful; lives would be more serenely enjoyable; and deaths would be delayed.

More importantly, love and human understanding would strongly increase because most personalities are striving unsuccessfully, somewhat, to be loved, recognized, wanted, needed, and respected by their fellow man.

www.ingramcontent.com/pod-product-compliance
Lightning Source LLC
Chambersburg PA
CBHW050524280326
41932CB00014B/2447